CW01510909

TELEMARKETING THAT WINS CUSTOMERS

Want to step up your telemarketing or
your teams? You need to read this first.

Shahida Afzal

trifle
solutions

Design by Clare McCabe www.purplestardesign.co.uk

DEDICATION

I dedicate this book to my sister Zaira, who believes in me and continuously encourages me to be the best I can, and to my Son's Deen & Feroz you both inspire me to do and achieve more, they constantly remind me of why I do what I do.

ACKNOWLEDGMENTS

I wish to express my heartfelt gratitude to my husband for letting me be, also my editor Jo Collie thank you for your perseverance and helping me to dig deep.

INDEX

FOREWORD

It's the most common problem telemarketing companies have: the never-ending churn of staff – coming and going through the proverbial revolving door. It costs money and time to train each one for a specific sales project only to have them disappear halfway through. I'm assuming that you're familiar and fed up with that issue as you've picked up this book.

The good news is that it really is possible to slow down that negative trend, if not stop it altogether. In the twenty-two years that I've run my own telemarketing business, I've targeted that problem, gnawing at it to get to the very core of the problem.

I found that it wasn't just one core problem; rather, it was a mix of several. By addressing each, one at a time, I started to see changes in my business. I noticed that they weren't peculiar to my business. In fact, every telemarketing company owner I knew that struggled with high staff turnover had these key issues at the root of their problem, too.

These key areas determine the health of your team and affect the behaviour of each member. I'm about to share them with you in this book. It excites me to think that the things that I've learned and now practice daily can help you, too, to find and keep your dream team.

The not so good news is that it takes a lot of commitment and dedication on your part to see the changes through. I'll be as transparent as possible, here: in my experience, there is no 'quick fix' to halt the staff churn. However, if your staff turnover has been eating away at your resources, costing you time and money for months or years, you can rest assured that your hard work will pay off.

Most business owners want to see results yesterday. It's time we broke down some of those longstanding, preconceived ideas about telemarketing: that there's quick, magic way to get strong leads and a fool proof method of getting your new team performing at its best in two weeks – that kind of unlikely claim.

The truth is that if you don't invest the time and carry out the process, you won't see the results you want. Many of us who profess to put relationships with our customers first don't actually spend enough time investing in building those relationships in the first place. It takes time to establish and cultivate a true relationship based on trust and confidence; they don't create themselves.

I learned this when I was in a previous telemarketing position, before I started my own telemarketing business. I had carefully invested a full year of my time in cultivating a relationship with a hard-to-reach customer and managed eventually to arrange a meeting between him and my boss. I practically begged for the meeting. Finally, when the big day arrived, my boss called me and told me to cancel it because he was running late.

I was hurt, upset and deeply unimpressed … and decided that I wouldn't make that call. How could he not know that the relationship I'd spent so much time and effort growing would be irrevocably damaged in one quick, dismissive call? All because my MD couldn't keep to his diary.

I left my job instead.

I had learned my first, clear lesson in 'nurturing', based on the understanding that the relationships between you and your team and between each member is not going to be formed in a week or two. It takes continuous learning.

When I was in my early twenties, I went on a package holiday to sunny Hawaii for eighteen to thirty-five year olds. On the way there, I stopped at a bookshop and bought my very first sales book - "The Twelve Cliches of Selling (And Why They Work" by Barry J. Farber (WORKMAN PUBLISHING COMPANY, 2001).   I remember my fellow travellers teasing me for my spending about five hours on the beach reading a personal development book.

I didn't mind. I could see that if I applied what I learned from the book, I'd be enjoying a lot more trips to Hawaii.

What I read in its pages changed my life. It left me in awe – even though none of it was particularly novel. In fact, it was all pretty basic stuff – a call to return to the fundamentals of how to sell well. It's so easy for us to forget the basics unless they're instilled in us by repetition.

I wanted to explore what I did for a living further. This title helped me to identify and understand the sales process that I was carrying out everyday. I understood how I ticked and began to see how I might improve and increase my sales.

It made such a difference to my work performance that I started to read all the books on telesales and self-development that I could lay my hands on and now have a library full of them ... but not one of them talks about how you should invest in your staff.

That's why I wanted to write this book. To put what I've discovered about building top, lasting sales teams into words and to plug that hole in the world of sales books.

The team that I have today is tight, happy, stable and committed. Each member makes my working life a wonderful experience and we've grown to care for each other. I wish you all the success and satisfaction at work that I enjoy – and to that end, may this book be the one self-help sales book you always remember and refer back to! Hopefully, you'll read it reclining on a sunny beach in Hawaii …

Here's to creating and keeping your strongest team -

Shahida

PART 1
RECRUITMENT

CHAPTER ONE
YOUR HIGH STAFF TURNOVER

"Quality performance starts with a positive attitude."
- Jeffrey Gitomer

There are a lot of business owners who speak about the failures of telemarketing and how "it just doesn't work". When I hear them, I know that they either don't realise or prefer not to admit that the error lay in the way they approached it, the lack of time they gave to the full process behind it.

In short, a failed telemarketing team or project comes down to a lack of patience rather than an implausible sales process. There are results available wherever you choose to research that show that telemarketing indeed can and does work – very effectively.

As with so many other worthwhile things in life, if you invest in something correctly from the beginning you will reap the rewards, but you need to be patient with it.

It comes down to your team, of course, and not just how well-trained or experienced each person in it is. You could have headhunted the best team in the world, but if it's not a good fit for your company or the interpersonal relationships are shallow, you'll either lose the team members or they'll underperform.

Let's shake up your circumstances and ask 'WHY' you are struggling with a high staff turnover and low sales performance. When we get to the root cause of the problem, you can deal with the symptoms one by one and prevent their arising again.

The Two Key Factors Affecting Staff Turnover

It's easy to see a pattern with high staff turnover when it emerges. You need to be able to identify the warning signs and know the solutions that you have at hand. There are many variables that can trigger it that may be unique to your business's situation, but it usually stems of one or both of two key things – and they both come into play at the very start of process:

- *Overselling the Sales Role*

- *A Core Values Mismatch between Your Business and Your Candidate*

If you rush the recruitment process, you do so at your peril. It's so much harder trying to put intrinsic issues right after you've employed someone.

Overselling the Sales Role

Most of us have fallen into the trap of trying to write exciting recruitment advertisement copy. The worst result, though, comes from 'overegging' it – making the role sound so much more than it really is. I have had much better success matching a candidate to a role with a straightforward, 'say what it does on the tin' approach to role advertising.

I tell them, "You will be doing the same one thing in excess of one hundred times a day." While that might not sound very appealing to most people, it's at least true. If you oversell the role, you'll inflate your candidates hopes, you'll end up with egg on your face and they'll run for the nearest exit. You'll both be disappointed.

If the copy is unclear or exaggerated, you're going to have some very disappointed interviewees to deal with. It's your time you're wasting, too, remember.

Keep it real. Manage your interviewees' expectations. That is a good, solid way to start your relationship and you'll save time replacing your candidate and retraining in the long run.

Core Values: Finding a Match for Your Business

This is the more difficult aspect to get right, as a person's individual values lie deep within them. They are mostly unconscious drives – affecting our behaviour all the time. We make our decisions based on our values, the things we hold to be important.

When you have a group of people together, they are grouping their personal values which give rise to a shared set of *core values*. Even if you haven't 'given' your team a set of company core values, it doesn't really matter. They already have a set that affect their group behaviour whether you like it or not. Some members may be more influential than others and it is the mix of those members of the group whose individual values will dictate the core values of the whole group.

They are prone to change, too, as they are held in the subconscious and not controlled by conscious thinking. They'll shift like sand, especially as members come and go, altering the group dynamic.

That's why it's so important for you to be clear what the core values of your business are before you start recruiting. You can't force anybody to take on your core values. What you can and should do, though, is to pick people who already have the majority of your core beliefs as their own individual values. In that way, you can protect your core beliefs and keep your business moving forwards in the direction you wish.

When you successfully select a group of people that share individual values, you stand a far better chance of creating a cohesive team that shares your business's core values. They will pull together naturally, without having to force themselves to do so. Nothing will disrupt your team as quickly as the addition of somebody who doesn't share the group's core values. Even if they have the most impressive sales record you've ever seen, if they're not a fit on the subconscious values level then you'll see problems arise soon within your team.

Core values can alter over time naturally. It's good for them to evolve as your business does.

They should not change your overall vision of the future, though. They're there to help you to keep track and cohesion of your team.

How do you recognise somebody that shares your values in the short amount of time an interview gives you, though?

Attracting the Right Person to Your Interview

As long as your advertisement is real and clear, you should already have weeded out a lot of interviewee mismatches before you even begin the process. You can relax a little more into asking the questions that will reveal their personality rather than qualifying their experience. At the end of the day, their CV should tell you if they have experience: you need to discover if they're a match.

Remember, you're not looking for another 'you' or to replicate anyone already on your team. While you may know their job inside and out, you need to find people who can complement you and the rest of the team. You're looking to have a variety of personalities to comprise your team ultimately – but each of them should hold your business's core values at heart. This should come out in conversation and we'll have a closer look at the interview process itself in the next chapter.

Keeping the Core Values In Place

Core values change over time. You should be able to tell by keeping in touch with each of your team members in regular appraisals.

How are they faring generally? How are they coping with their workload and ongoing training? How are they getting along with everybody else in the team? This isn't just down to KPIs. This is more about establishing their feelings and if their individual values still resonate with the business's core values.

Don't always believe what they say at first. People often 'screen' their true feelings when they feel at risk in some way – their job may be in danger, for example. This is precisely why it's so important that you spend as much time as you can to build your relationships with each member of your team. Communication is all-important: each of them has to feel and truly know that a one-to-one with you is a safe place for them to speak.

Everybody has a bad day or two at some point, so bear in mind that you're looking for a trend in a person's behaviour. Don't leap on one or two things that may have happened over a week or so, especially if there are outside influences in play, such as family or health concerns. You're looking for the way a person behaves and is around others over a protracted length of time. If they don't meet their KPIs and do not seem to have your business's core values at heart, then you are likely dealing with someone who doesn't fit. Even worse, sometimes they hit all of their KPIs with ease and still don't fit in with the team, which can be wholly disrupted by their behaviour.

Do the right thing for them and the rest of your team and let them go. They will be happier somewhere else where they fit better with the business and team; you will stand a better chance of keeping on track more quickly without them.

CHAPTER TWO

THE INTERVIEW PROCESS

"The real opportunity for success lies within the person and not the job." Zig Ziglar

The key to a successful interview is *focus*. If you have taken good care with your candidate search, advertising campaign and shortlisting, you should be left with a handful of qualified candidates. You don't need to waste time talking with them about their CVs; you should know by this stage if they have the skills for the job.

The Previous Experience Trap

Although it's good to have a glowing record - and let's hope that most of your recruits can offer you one - is it really the be all and end all of your search? If you put all your hopes into somebody with a glorious past, don't be entirely surprised if they don't match your glorious hopes for the future.

16

Their past does not equal their present, much less your combined future. What really matters is their ability to absorb what you're saying and to take on the culture of your business swiftly. Are they adaptable? Can they apply their learned skills to a brand new set up?

There's a point to be made about experience, here: while it is helpful to bring into the team a member who already has call confidence, they'll be no good for your team if they are not flexible enough to relearn some aspects of the job your way. Personally, I prefer taking on new team members with no previous experience – completely green. I find it easier to train someone my way without having ingrained problem practices to undo and unlearn.

I remember being shocked at how below par ninety per cent of the telemarketers I interviewed were. Some thought it was acceptable to swear on the phone, and I vividly recall the morning I heard one of them call the CEO of a FYSE 500 company 'darling'.

Have some exercises ready for them to go through with you in the interview. It's a good

17

way to separate the sheep from the goats in the 'previous experience' field. For instance, you may be surprised at how few people have any concept of what thorough note taking entails. On their CV, they may call themselves 'an excellent telemarketer' – this is a good way for you to see how many of those are willing to pick up the phone to make a call in front of you.

Unless you have a very specific area of experience that you're looking for in a candidate, rather focus the interview time on your finding out if this person is a good fit for your business. You are looking to achieve a better understanding of their personality and motivations in this instance.

Questions and Expectations

Don't be afraid to ask questions that require them to really have done their homework. Feel free to ask things such as:

"What do you know about the company? Why are you looking to progress your career in this particular field?"

"What are the key differences in working with us and where you were before?"

18

"Why do you want to join us?

"Ultimately, why do you want a career in telemarketing or telesales? What is it about the work that really makes you tick?"

I expect applicants to look at our case studies and our testimonials before their interview. These days, your information should be easily available to them on multi social media channels.

Very often, though, the applicant will withdraw their application on being asked these questions. That's alright with me: it tells me that they were applying for 'just a job' rather than the experience of being part of a great team. I'd rather get the right sort of person join us in the first instance than to have to weed them out of the team later.

People who have really thought about applying have fluid answers for these questions, which helps enormously. From the very first day, you can begin to see what their motivators are. The desire for emotional attachment and human connection with a team starts with them and is as clear as daylight. That helps you to form your plan on how to manage them as individuals and subsequently the team as whole. If they have that natural self-motivation, all they need is a nudge to go in the right direction.

This calls for your investing some time and analysing their results a lot more in the beginning.

Motivation

Look beyond what you know. Don't go into the interview with preconceptions and a skewed perspective of the person you're interviewing based on what you wish they'd be like.

Everyone gets motivated by different things, so don't make the mistake I did in my early years of thinking that your team is motivated by purely money. I had a surprise when I finally asked them during appraisals and one-to-ones.

For a team leader, the biggest motivator is to see the team do well, knowing that it was due to their successful leadership.

For agents, the reward of public acknowledgement is the greatest motivator. Praise and recognition in front of the team goes a long way to inspiring bigger and better performances. It encourages the human connection and relationships between each of the team members – which is why your nurturing your team is so important.

I have had the pleasure of working with some staff members whose own standards were so high that just five hours' of their time was worth the average agent's full day in terms of results. Two of them I remember vividly would get themselves into a real state of anxiety if they felt that they couldn't deliver exemplary results continually.

"What's the problem?" I'd ask them. "You've over-delivered and yet you seem to be really on edge and frustrated. What's going on?"

"I might have achieved the result but I know it wasn't done quite right," would be the usual reply. These high standards were self-imposed – the key motivators for these particular people. No amount of encouragement from management could have improved their performance; they were tougher on themselves than anyone. Their core beliefs were so strong that those were the only motivators that they needed.

It might sound like a dream scenario but managing their stress levels became the new challenge. You need your team to be calm and happy as well as results orientated.

The Three Whys

An effective way of cutting through the 'previous experience' part of the interviewing process is to focus on your candidate's personal history. Ask them about a decision they've made in the past, allow them to answer and then keep digging:

"That's interesting ... why did you do that?"

Repeat this three times, phrasing yourself slightly differently each time ... and then you'll have a better idea of the mindset of the person involved. You'll also know if they can think on their feet quickly enough for the role.

This will offer you a picture of what motivates them, if they have the all-important balance between IQ and EQ (we'll look at that more in depth in Part 3) that they'll need to be a part of a team with clear core values in place.

Transparency

If you have time enough in the interview, it's a good opportunity to raise an initial question about the candidate's 'Five Year Plan'. If they don't have one, you might suggest that you can work on it together during their training stage if they get the job.

There are two good reasons for doing this. Firstly, it helps you to understand more deeply what they're all about, not just professionally but personally, too. The plan should cover personal as well as career goals. If you can find ways in which it echoes your business's own 'Five Year Plan', you're off to a great start on developing a new staff member who fits in with your team as they share common core values.

Secondly, it offers you the opportunity to be transparent with them about where you'd like to take the business and to show them how they can play a part in its progress over a long period. It instils confidence and a sense of belonging to the team on the part of the candidate.

Outside of the interview process, I have found that to have a visible, illustrative chart of the business's longterm plan in the office area helps to keep everybody focused and moving in the same direction. Likewise, a chart showing who's who on the team and where they sit in the workflow is very helpful in cutting down on communication breakdowns.

Many companies don't like to do this, but I have found that the transparency is appreciated and respected. Many people relate better to something they can actually see in front of them, so share it at the earliest stage.

The Money Issue

In telemarketing, it's always true that if 'you buy cheap, you buy twice'.

Don't scrimp on your offer of salary. Pay the right candidate what their time and skills are worth and do it gladly. Keep your end goal in mind, and ask yourself, "Who am I measuring my results against?"

If you're pricing yourself in the market properly, there's no need to hesitate in paying better fees. That way, you'll get better candidates wanting to work with you in the first place.

At the start of my own business, I was undercharging my customers considerably. I see now with hindsight that I didn't quite understand how much effort it takes to really get a good, qualified opportunity. I was over-delivering; because my standard of work was so high, my customers were getting a platinum service for bronze prices. For months, I couldn't understand why I was so busy!

If you price yourself right with your customer, you can afford to pay your team right.

You're asking for someone's commitment to your end goal, so be sure that you know what their commitment should comprise and exactly what you're going to offer in return. If you don't have this clarity from the very start, your relationship with your team members will be stunted. Neither you nor they will be clear on what the job is ultimately about, your team won't believe that you value or even respect them and you will never know if they're giving you the best of themselves or not.

'Market Ready' versus 'Sales Ready'

A lot of the people that you will get to interview will be those who are well-versed in getting 'marketing-ready opportunites' as opposed to 'sales-ready opportunities'. There's a big difference between the two, and there are two different skillsets required for each of them.

Some people who do the former will never be ready to perform the latter. Others recognise sales-ready opportunities straightaway and act on them. Whichever one you need will depend on the project at hand.

Over the years, the term 'telemarketing' has become a blanket term that covers both areas of call marketing and sales, which include:

- Making customers aware of a product or service

- Lead generation

- Contacting existing customers

- Providing information

- Carrying out market research

- Selling products and services to both new and existing customers

Keep in mind, though, that the two are very distinctly different and you need to find out which skills your candidate has before you employ them, depending on the project. I would say that:

CALL MARKETING creates awareness, interest, sales opportunities and informs, analyses feedback. It covers making appointments and lead generation.

CALL SALES is the actual sale of a product or service to a customer – the close of the deal.

In both roles, a candidate should be able to see how much more can be achieved from each call and not settle for less. This may mean that fewer calls are made than your target number, but the quality of the longer calls should make up for the quantity of those made in a day.

As a guide to help you with the interview process, here are examples of job descriptions and interview questions that I have developed over time and use today. Take from them as you wish, although you might like to add or subtract from them according to your own company's core values or specific project.

JOB DESCRIPTION FOR TELEMARKETER ROLE

Objective of role: To undertake calls and administration to fulfil client campaigns.

Responsibilities:

- To make scripted phone calls as directed by the Telemarketing Team Leader

- To conduct administration to support calls made, for example, follow-up emails

- To read information and research provided to ensure understanding of individual projects

- To undertake training as required to maintain performance in role

- To raise problems/issues/opportunities with Telemarketing Team leader

- To provide support for telemarketing colleagues as required

- To attend monthly/weekly team meetings

- To provide administrative support for the Telemarketing team as required

- Other reasonable tasks as required by the role

Behaviours:

- Putting the client first

- Dare to think differently

- Step up and take responsibility

- One team

- Be professional

- Embrace change

- Communicate effectively

Measurements of success:

- Meeting project KPIs, e.g., on calls made and qualified opportunities generated depending on the individual campaign

INTERVIEW QUESTIONS FOR TELEMARKETER ROLE

This should be a pre-booked call when you have already explained to them that this will take up to thirty minutes. They should be sitting somewhere quiet where they can concentrate and the phone signal is good.

Start by explaining the job (in brief) and the interview process. Say something like:

"We'll work through this telephone interview together and then I'll answer any questions you have about the role.

"If we both decide that we would like to progress your application, the next stage is to come in for a trial with us so that you can see the workplace and what is involved. You will be paid for that. How does that sound?"

Follow on with open questions, such as:

- Tell me about yourself

- What appeals to you about this job? When you saw the advert – what made you apply?

- What do you know about (YOUR COMPANY)?

- What other sort of jobs are you applying for?

- Why are you looking for a new job?

- Why did you leave your last job(s)? (This needs to be asked for last two or three jobs – is there a pattern/area of concern?)

- What is your current salary? What is your notice period?

- Where do you live? How will you get here everyday?

- What has been your favourite job? Why?

What did you enjoy about it?

- What did you like least about your last job?

- Can you give me an example of something you have had to learn on the job? How did you do that? Could you talk me through the process?

- Have you ever received one-to-one coaching and training "on the job"? Tell me about that.

- Can you give me an example of a time that you have received negative feedback? How did you deal with that? How did it make you feel?

- What is the most difficult person/customer you have had to deal with? Why were they difficult and how did you handle the situation?

- What's the toughest thing you have ever had to do? The hardest you have had to try? (This might be something personal, something at school or work)

- Can you give me an example of a time when you have been busy with lots to do and have had to prioritise to fit everything in? Talk me through how you did that?

- Can you give me an example of a time when

31

you have been under pressure and how you dealt with it?

- How do you feel about ongoing training and development at work?

- What is your biggest strength?

- What is your biggest weakness?

- What are your career goals?

- Lastly, how do you like to be managed?

JOB DESCRIPTION FOR TELEMARKETER TEAM LEADER ROLE

Objective of role:

To manage the day-to-day tasks of the Telemarketers to ensure that campaigns are run successfully according to the client's needs.

Responsibilities:

- To manage the daily tasks of the team

- To monitor individual and team performance

- To set goals and monitor progress against team and individual KPIs and goals with the telemarketers

- To monitor call quality by listening to calls and providing feedback

- To manage work schedules on a weekly basis and make sure there is enough resource for each campaign

- To manage and communicate data for the team in a format that everyone can stick to and follow to facilitate clear reporting

- To work with the Client Services Executive to understand client requirements and then produce a project sheet and communicate it to the telemarketers

- To hold weekly catch up meetings with the telemarketers

- To look for ways to improve the performance of each telemarketer and provide on-the-job training and guidance

- To help the telemarketers with any problems they may have in the workplace

- To report back to the Client Services Executive with weekly/fortnightly reports on their campaigns

- To lead recruitment for telemarketers, with

the support of other managers

- To ensure project sheets are up to date and readable for the telemarketers

- To manage sickness, absence, holidays, appraisals and performance discussions for the telemarketers

- Other reasonable tasks as required by the role

Behaviours:

- Putting the client first
- Dare to think differently
- Step up and take responsibility
- One Trifle team
- Be professional
- Embrace change
- Communicate effectively
- Lead people

Measurements of success:

- Meeting team and individual KPIs
- Appraisals Undertaken

CHAPTER THREE
GETTING THE 'TEAM FIT' RIGHT

"Fortune favors the bold." -Virgil

At the risk of my telling you what you think is the obvious, you'd be as surprised as I have been to discover how few telemarketing business owners distinguish between their hiring a 'marketing ready' candidate and someone who's 'sales ready'.

As we covered in the previous chapter, the two are completely different roles; when they get muddled up at the very start, there's no hope of the interviewee's being the right fit for the team.

To clarify, marketers identify qualified leads and prepare the way for the sales team to close the deal by creating or increasing interest in the product. They cut down on the need for endless cold calling and increase the likelihood of a successful sales campaign. They are skilled at setting appointments and have a natural, easy manner on lead calls.

Salespeople are good at just that: they close the deal and find it easier to do so if the marketing campaign has prepared the way for them. As long as the lead is qualified and interested and the sales person is experienced and empathic, the deal is ready to be closed.

Good marketers do not always make great salespeople and vice versa, although occasionally you might come across someone who can do both. They are very different tasks which require very different skillsets.

The proof of the pudding is in the eating, as they say: you'll only know for sure if you've made the right choice after time has passed. Of course, you'll keep an eagle eye on your new recruit all the way through probation and need to have a clear idea of what traits you should be looking for – both positive and negative.

While it may feel uncomfortable to keep a checklist for human behaviour, I use my own as a good starting point. After all, this is a business you're running, not a social group.

Of course, each business has different needs and not all of the following may seem crucial for you to find in your telemarketing team members. It's a good place to start, though, as it has been compiled over many years specifically to build and refine my own team.

PUTTING THE CLIENT FIRST

This is Number One on the list of things each of your team members should hold close at heart. Without this and an ability to empathise with the customers and clients, a campaign will not get off the ground.

Positive signs:

- Thinks about the consequences of their actions and decisions for the client

- Asks the client questions to define their expectations

- Learns what is important for the client

- Shows empathy to the client – puts themselves in the client's shoes

- Identifies client problems to be fixed

- Actively demonstrates that they care about meeting the client's needs

Negative signs:

- Complains when asked to "go the extra mile" for a client

- Does not seek to understand client needs

- Takes an overly hardsell approach

- Doesn't listen effectively to the client

- Doesn't follow up on conversations to show the client that they care

- Does not define what a clear lead looks like

DARING TO THINK DIFFERENTLY

Showing initiative when it's appropriate is one of the key things that makes a successful team.

Positive signs:

- Analyses past events to find solutions to client problems

- In decisions, balances the needs of your

company and the client

- Looks at problems from different angles

- Puts quality first

- Demonstrates initiative

- Challenges where things could be done differently

Negative signs:

- Does not take responsibility for resolving problems/overcoming challenges

- Doesn't use data or information to make decisions

- Doesn't consider the end goal when making decisions

- Doesn't look for different ways to solve problems

TAKING RESPONSIBILITY

This is a quality that needs to be nurtured in some people more than others. When a person is confident at work, though, their capacity to take responsibility grows enormously.

Positive signs:

- Is resilient and tenacious to overcome challenges and achieve goals

- Admits when they don't know the answer but takes responsibility to find it

- Asks questions to learn

- Holds themselves and others accountable

- Steps up to make the right decision if no-one else is around to do it

Negative signs:

- Gives up or doesn't make an effort to get things done

- Makes assumptions rather than using processes or facts

- Makes the same mistake over and over and doesn't learn from it

- Doesn't ask for help

- Doesn't back up their decisions with data, information or evidence

BEING A TEAM MEMBER

Usually a difficult one to quantify as it means different things to different teams. Here are some points that I stick to – you might wish to add your own.

Positive signs:

- Shares successes with others in the team

- Supports others in their successes

- Gives colleagues positive feedback

- Shares knowledge to benefit the team

- Treats people with respect

- Motivates and inspires confidence in the team around them

Negative signs:

- Doesn't say "good morning" to their colleagues at the start of the day

- Is negative when given feedback

- Is self-orientated

- Doesn't step in to help colleagues when they're under pressure

BEING PROFESSIONAL

The very basic prerequisites of any candidate, although remember that someone who's new to a professional environment needs more lassitude, support and patience on your part.

Positive signs:

- Turns up on time

- Plans their time using tools that work for them

- Systemises when it's appropriate

- Knows when and why to ask questions, and to whom

- Uses different support mechanisms to demonstrate calm under pressure

- Acknowledges own and others' frustrations

- Takes every opportunity to demonstrate they want to do a good job

- Monitors own performance

Negative signs:

- Doesn't show flexibility to make up time lost

- Doesn't prioritise effectively

- Doesn't use the tools provided – e.g. project sheet, web page etc – when making calls

- Takes challenges from callers personally and takes frustrations onto the next call

- Rushes to get people off the phone

- Doesn't think about the impact of their actions on others

EMBRACING CHANGE

The longer a person is working with you and your team, the greater the capacity for them to become stuck in their ways. It's a human trait, not a personal black mark … but keep your eyes and ears open to it and coax them out of it as much as possible.

Positive signs:

- Looks out for "red flags" – things that will identify when change is needed

- Demonstrates awareness of the need to change
- Demonstrates a flexible approach when processes change
- Identifies how change can happen without detracting from your company's core values
- Keeps talking to people through change

Negative signs:

- "Shoots people down in flames" when they suggest changes
- Doesn't air their own thoughts about change
- Pushes for change for the sake of it
- Resists change
- Resists opportunities to learn – keeps doing what they've always done, even if it's not the right thing

COMMUNICATING EFFECTIVELY

While a team member might have a great call manner, their easy communication may not extend naturally to the rest of the team.

Positive signs:

- Demonstrates assertive and positive body language

- Uses a positive and assertive tone of voice

- Builds rapport

- Listens, summarises and recaps

- Demonstrates empathy

- Clearly and concisely communicates what needs to be done

- Adapts language to get their message to land effectively

Negative signs:

- Doesn't make eye contact or show that they're listening

- Waffles, mumbles or otherwise lacks clarity in communication

- Doesn't ask questions to get to the root of issues quickly

STRATEGIC THINKING

Is it asking too much to have your candidate offer more than just one skill? I think not. If your team is to work as a cohesive force, each member needs to be able to think a few steps ahead.

Positive signs:

- Contributes to the strategic objectives of the organisation and department

- Researches new opportunities that could contribute to the organisation's strategic objectives

- Approaches short-term operational issues with a long-term perspective

- Regularly feeds back to senior management on issues that may impact the organisation's strategic objectives

- Ensures that individuals' and team objectives clearly reflect the organisation's strategic objectives

Negative signs:

- Takes a short-term view, only focusing on the issue in front of them

- Is reactive rather than proactive

- Fails to keep up with what's going on in the broader industry

- Does not clearly communicate the strategic vision to team members

- Does not identify threats and opportunities for the business

LEADING OTHERS

Not everybody is a natural leader but there are some skills latent to leadership that everyone can be trained to use.

Positive signs:

- Takes responsibility for team performance

- Delegates appropriately

- Coaches and mentors team members

- Inspires and motivates others to perform

- Demonstrates self-awareness

- Promotes diversity and inclusion

- Helps people in the team to learn from mistakes

Negative signs:

- Avoids challenging conversations

- Does not help team members to identify training and development opportunities

- Creates a blame culture

- Does not identify own strengths or weaknesses or seek to mitigate these

- Does not ensure team members have clear targets to achieve

Over time, this list will help you decide if you have the right people on your team. If you decide that you have, then the next thing is to work on keeping them with you. It's time to discover everyone's "Five Year Plan" and to create a way that you can nurture them, support them and help them to achieve it.

CHAPTER FOUR
UNDOING BAD HABITS

"Motivation will almost always beat mere talent." -
Norman Ralph Augustine

You've gone through the interview process, paying close attention to the personality of the candidate and being circumspect about the glowing comments on the CV. You've offered them the job – congratulations! It's time to start the training process from Day One.

Anyone who does a repetitive task day after day should get the hang of it pretty quickly. If you wait too long before you show them that there are ten variables of that one thing that might happen repeatedly, you'll frustrate your new recruit. Best to get the training in from the very start.

Suddenly, all sorts of niggling things start

50

to crop up – and the majority of them come from the 'Previous Experience' clause we talked about earlier. As I say, this is the main reason why I really enjoy taking on a new recruit who's had little to no experience before they come to me. It takes much more time and persuasion to get somebody to agree to 'unlearn' bad habits; often, they don't agree that they are bad habits in the first place.

Here are some of those that you might discover in your own business and some ideas on how you can stop them from becoming bigger issues later.

The Three Standards of Early Training

Normally, when someone is doing the same thing day in and day out, you'll quickly find out which are the areas that need your training focus.

A new team member might have experience and great knowledge, but once they've started out with you they need to have an open mind and to be prepared to 'unlearn' some habits they may have formed over their career so far.

You can expect them to know the basics – for

instance, that this is a volume game and they need to acquire a certain amount of leads in a given timeframe. There will be a lot of 'no answer' calls, 'numbers not in service' calls and a lot of 'call back' responses. How they go about dealing with those and getting the leads, though, is ultimately going to reflect on you ... so make sure that they carry your business's core beliefs and values at heart.

If you make time to sit with your new team member, you will end up training in real time – while they are in motion and learning, rather than after the fact. This makes the best use of their probationary period and will save you a lot of potential headaches later, when it's too late to make changes to the team. Make sure that you prioritise time with them in your diary for when they start and stick to it.

The more time you spend with your new team members when they start, the more easily you'll identify the patterns of potential problem areas. They tend to arise in three main areas:

- *Experience*: the muddy waters of 'previous experience' in which may dwell all manner of nasty surprises

- *Motivation*: although your new recruit may be excited at the start, are they still keen three months into probation? Are they growing with the role or shying away from it?

- *Commitment*: how willing is your new team member proving to bring more to the role than just the basic requirements? Are they willing to 'go the extra mile' for the rest of the team and the project?

With each of these three, you'll see them flourish or fail very quickly. There will be telltale signs along the way. Make sure you pay attention to the warning signs.

The Matter of Empathy

When someone is on the phone in the first few weeks of their being with you, they're usually nervous. Quite apart from their being on a call to a stranger, which is enough to cause anyone a degree of anxiety, they're working with a brand new team.

We're all human. There's always an underlying psychological reason why somebody is grappling with a concept. Remember, you were a blank page once, too ... somebody nurtured you and took time to teach you before you became who you are today. You received the passion to develop yourself from somebody else: now it's your opportunity to pass that passion on.

Not everybody has the good fortune to be nurtured early in life. The will to survive is what gets a lot of people through, and while that can generate enough energy to progress in life it sometimes lacks the tools of refinement: how to phrase oneself, how to approach a subject tactfully, how to show empathy without being overbearing.

It doesn't mean the person is bad at his job, though.

Yes, there will be times when you'll have a telemarketer who's simply not on your path, but as a manager you have to take responsibility for the majority of performance within your team.

It usually comes down to you: what are you doing to support this person? It's all too easy to point the finger, but at the end of the day your team's performance is a reflection of you – of your recruitment process through to training.

Take time to step into your new team member's shoes. Resolve to walk the next five years in them.

Warning Signs in Behaviour Patterns

Once you're in an empathic leadership frame of mind, you can decipher the clues that come your way as you sit with your new recruit.

Note, though, that there needs to be a degree of compromise: sometimes, good enough is fine. What 'good enough' translates as has to be decided between the team and management. If you can see that the right effort has been made then there's no need for a "crucial conversation".

Back to those warning signs – which will show up. It's up to you to notice them. Here are those that I have discovered most frequently.

Not Reading The Script

When a new recruit doesn't use the script or other tools they've been given it's usually because they're filling in gaps due to nervousness or lack of knowledge about the product or service.

They don't have the answer in the forefront of

their minds, so they improvise. They panic. While initiative can be a good thing, in this case it can be counteractive and it accumulates towards the end of the month when they end up with no leads, meetings or appointments. They miss their KPIs.

This usually happens when a relatively seasoned telemarketer gets so over-familiar with the script that they stop looking at it, thinking that they have it verbatim. The trouble is, they tend to memorise sections of it, not all of it.

If the majority of their calls deal with issues that are commonly repeated, they'll aptly deal with the questions that come up. If they get a curve ball, though, they're literally lost for words. They'll ramble over it. Important bits of information may be left out altogether.

The script is a tool to be used. In an ideal world, we don't want each call to sound contrived or 'read'. However, if not using it means that important cues are missed, we do what we can to make sure that the team respects the script.

If you have spent time on your telemarketers' script, you didn't compose it to look pretty. Even if there's a project that your recruit has been on for six months, one day they will have a question that they've never had before for which they need an answer to hand.

Make sure that every team member has the script open in front of them when they're making the call. Assumption is a really dangerous thing! They must never assume that they know all there is to know about the product or service they're selling, even if they've been selling it for months on end. They must stick to the script.

Apart from anything else, the customer has not authorised anybody to sell it 'their' way. There's a definitive way the customer wants the product or service sold. So, if a telemarketer has blagged it and made up a unique version of a sales pitch, you won't have a leg to stand on when it comes to explaining to the customer what went wrong in the call. You wouldn't want to send the recording of such a call to the customer.

Sloppy Note Taking

Sometimes, new recruits with previous experience bring less than desirable habits with them. They might write brief notes following a call that are simply erroneous.

For example, for a brief conversation that goes as follows:

"Good morning - who is the person who buys your IT products?"

"I'm sorry, he doesn't take calls."

... I've seen agents write "not interested" as call notes.

Of course, they don't know at all if the buyer is interested as they haven't managed to speak to them yet. The call was inconclusive and the assumption lazy. In this instance, you can tell that they have been trained in the past to make as many calls as possible to hit a numerical target only. They might make a couple of hundred calls a day but the quality of the calls is abysmal.

We spend a lot of time unbreaking those habits to a point of sitting down with them and reworking their mindset. It takes a fair time to do this as old habits die hard; the practice might be firmly ingrained by that stage. With repetition and patience, though, an agent can learn new skills.

If we've managed to recruit somebody who

has corresponding core beliefs to our core values as a company, it takes less time to achieve. It saves a lot of angst, too.

Being Too Afraid to Ask

Often, a team member might miss cues and guides because they're simply too afraid to ask a question that they think is embarrassing or 'dumb'.

As a manager, you then hold their hand through the learning process, whether your team member is brand new or not. The question to ask to pre-empt this predicament is simply, "How do you like to learn?"

Active listening and real empathy cuts through the posturing and insecurities that so often accompanies new additions to your telemarketing team.

How much are you willing to invest in your recruit? The temptation may be to let them get on with it, learn from the others and glean what they can … but they're on your payroll, after all. If you want the best from them that they clearly want to give, you need to invest your time and 'handhold' for a while.

Alternatively, you may have to hold back on dictating and let them lead you in how they can best learn the information and relay it persuasively. It's not your way or the highway: to reach your shared goal, you need to work together.

Unique Acronyms

When you take on somebody who has had previous experience in telemarketing, the chances are high that they've come across and worked with acronyms that differ to the ones you use.

It's such an easy thing to sort out from the start, but I've seen it happen many times. The same acronym can mean different things to different teams, so it's up to you to make sure that everyone is using the same ones.

"otq" (opportunity to qualify), "cb" (call back), "ni" (no interest) – they all seem so clear when it's spelled out like that, but are you sure that everyone is clear what yours mean?

It takes time to get everybody on the same page. You need to get onto that straightaway, though; if you leave it for a month then it will be too late to avoid a huge mix up of information. Your new recruits may have been using their learned acronyms while the rest of the team are using the correct ones.

You can imagine the consequences of miscommunication that can follow. If you sit with the new person every day for a short while from the very start of their employment with you, it will seem like a 'transition' period that you're steering them through. Rather that than a mountainous problem to tackle and sort out after a month of letting them blithely do things their own way, in discord with the rest of the team.

Be Transparent

Every single day, be clear with your team members about what they can expect. Tell them what will be reviewed, what they will be measured on, what their one-to-ones will be about ... then, the day after, rinse and repeat.

Your telemarketers have one thing to do: the call. The way they're going to learn to do it well is by listening and repeating.

There's no real formula, but the closest thing to one would be:

listen + repeat back what you've heard + apply

When things go awry with my own team, I remind them that "My problem isn't that it happened, it's that you didn't feel that you could come to me and tell me you didn't understand in the first place."

They shouldn't be afraid of asking questions. Every person on your team should have the confidence to ask even what they may feel is a 'dumb' question. There really is no such thing as a 'dumb' question. If they feel intimidated, they're not going to feel free to ask a question … and that one question might be the one that, left unanswered, will lead to a poor call.

If you give your new team member a really strong foundation, then it nips most of the problems in the bud.

"I love you as my team member, but I don't like the way you did such and such …" is a fair and constructive way of training your telemarketers. It's a bit like parenting. If you know something is wrong, bring it to the table rather than stew on it for a couple of weeks.

Commit to nurturing your new team members from Day One. Spend time understanding how they work, as well as what factors made life easy in their previous roles. People respond well when they feel that they've really been listened to.

Which brings us on to the most effective team-growing and securing tool of all - *Nurturing*, which is so important that it's the focus of the next part of this book.

CHAPTER 4-UNDOING BAD HABITS

PART 2
NURTURING

CHAPTER FIVE
YOUR TEAM'S BESPOKE TRAINING PLAN

"Whether you think you can or you think you can't, you're right." - Henry Ford

In the years that I've spent learning how to get the very best results from my team consistently, this is what I've found to be true:

Everybody likes to be taught differently.

Well, of course. It's to be expected ... after all, we're all unique individuals. Thanks to both Nature and Nurture, we've developed our own inimitable ways of communicating with others and performing in a sales environment.

As desirable as a bespoke training regime would be, however, achieving it sounds like an impossible challenge. Your day is full enough already. Where will you find the hours to develop numerous ways of training each and every member of your staff? It's impractical – if not impossible, surely?

Don't panic: it's not as imposing an obstacle as it sounds.

Different Ways to Deliver the Same Programme

Firstly, it's important to remember that you don't need to rethink the information you want to teach. What you're aiming to do is to find the right way of delivering the same material to each team member.

Immediately, that should make the task feel much easier. It means that you are perfectly capable of training every team member the required skillset successfully based on what you know already. You know your product inside and out.

The missing link for you lies hidden within the person you're training. There's really only one way to discover it …

"What Do You Want? What Do You Need?"

In Part 1, we looked at how your sourcing and

employing the right candidate was crucial for the success of your whole team. Finding out their 'why' at that stage was important in order for you to decide whether or not they shared your company's core values. If they did, they were likely to be a good fit, irrespective of their aptitude. Their *attitude* at that point was more important. Remember, a set of skills can be taught; aspects of someone's personality is deeply rooted and less pliable.

Now that they're on-board, though, it's their *aptitude* that needs to be polished and sustained. Their skillset needs broadening and their initiative encouraged for the sake of the whole team.

When you think about it, it's a good thing that everybody has different skills and temperaments to bring to the job. Were everyone the same, you'd not only have lots of people on board with exactly the same strengths but the same weak points, too. That could be disastrous.

Ideally, your team should complement each other - fill in the gaps for each other both skills and personality-wise. One team member's weakness could be another's forte. They should be aware of each other's strengths as well as their own, so that they can operate as a team fluidly and with confidence.

When you recognise your team's skills and reward their winning moments, you actively encourage them to stay. Studies have shown that people tend to want to stay in jobs that make them happy and edify them rather than for the salary.

Invest Your Time to Nurture Your Team

Booking more time in your diary to spend with each member of your team may seem an impossible dream on the face of it … you're already booked up to the hilt. Just think, though, what it could cost you if you don't.

It's far safer and more cost effective to develop an existing member of your team from their current position to a more senior role than to gamble on hiring someone unknown from outside the company. It would take ages to train an outsider on everything concerning the company, the role and your expectations of their performance.

By now, you have worked alongside your team member and know that their core values and work ethic is strong; it's only their skillset that needs expanding. What's more, they've worked alongside the rest of the team, too, and they respect and trust each other.

Now is the time to encourage them to really excel in their career by empowering them to grow and succeed. What are they passionate about? How can you trigger that passion in them at work for them to want to conquer the new skillset they need for the role? Spending more time with them, one-to-one in appraisal meetings is key to your being able to motivate and support them as they need.

You don't have to go overboard on the ideas – I stick to small tasks for them to do and fun rewards as it all has to be budgeted, but I always enjoy a great return on investment!

We also have a small 'gift table' in the office, laden with chocolate bars, bottles of wine, soaps and other treats by the team leader, who's given a small monthly budget to splash out on it. We aim to always have a minimum of ten gifts on it so that everyone has a bit of choice.

Every week, the agent with the best wrap time or similar achievement gets to pick their own treat from the gift table. There is a weekly trophy, too, complete with mini award ceremony each Friday for the best team performer of the week. All of these treats and regular public accolades fosters friendly competition between the team members and raises the happy mood in the office.

We have a pizza Wednesday every other week, a monthly award for 'Employee of The Month' and a team lunch, to which everybody brings in a dish of their own. Eating together is always a bonding time. We have a quarterly lunch outing to a restaurant, where the team member with the most 'wins' has to make a speech.

I also make use of a 'Theme of the Month' – for example, ask for a referral on every call, or ask what the buyer is doing for Valentine's Day on every call. It helps to break the repetition of the call sheet and to fully engage the caller with the buyer, making an otherwise standard call far more memorable and personal.

Of course, birthdays are always to be celebrated. I bring in a cake (please don't expect the birthday boy or girl to have to do that themselves!), we decorate their station before they arrive and I order in lunch for everyone.

Lastly, a small gesture that I adopted years ago that I have learned makes a big difference to office life is thanking the team at the end of every single day. It takes very little effort to do and pays dividends to morale. It doesn't take long for the job to feel stale and like a drudge without the manager's acknowledgement and respect. I rate this as so important that I tell my team leaders to prioritise it. If they forget to do anything during the day, it had better not be that!

You don't have to throw huge amounts of money at things to make people feel wanted.

Personal Development

There was a time when the phrase 'personal development at work' was considered a fanciful, watery concept. You were expected to accept your role, to keep your head down and get on with it. If you didn't like it or stuck your head above the parapet (especially if you were female) then you should leave.

Thankfully, change is the one constant in life.

These days, you'd be hard pressed to find a

company with a solid staff complement that didn't invest very seriously in 'personal development'. The encouragement of employees to better their lives through exploring their talents, personality, goals and abilities is expected of companies now.

It benefits everybody. For you, it means a happier, more solid team and an end to your fears that your best-trained people will be lured away by a competitor as long as you embrace it. Happy team members are long-lasting team members.

Appraisals and Regular Training

Have a look at the way your business is organised. Do you offer development opportunities for your team members across the board? Is there enough chance for growth and variation for them in-house to keep them interested and engaged? Does your company attract higher quality applicants from outside?

Research suggests that by 2025, seventy-five per cent of the workforce will comprise millennials (www.forbes.com). The vast majority of that age group says that the opportunity at work for 'personal development' is the most important factor in their job searching.

Do you have opportunities set up for your team for personal development? If not, here are some solid starter points for your own in-house programme:

How to Encourage Personal Growth in Your Company

Remember, this is not a programme that you're putting in place primarily for your own company's benefit. This has to be for your team. It's all about nurturing each of them to stretch, challenge themselves and to find success in achievable tasks. For every milestone they pass, they will feel edified, positive and more confident. As a manager, you will see the immeasurable benefits of this very quickly. You'll wonder why you hadn't tried it before!

Ask each of your employees what they want and need at work to make their time there enjoyable. This is best done in conversation, of course, but there's no reason why you shouldn't make use of a simple questionnaire, too, to get the juices flowing. Once they've filled that out, make a time to sit together privately in one-to-one meetings.

Use 'active listening' in those meetings. Start a plan that's unique to each of them that focuses just on personal growth and career development. This is separate from their job descriptions; it's based entirely on your discussions with them about what they want for their lives.

What are their goals, and why do they want to achieve them? Will their achieving them help them to enjoy the lifestyle they want to create? Will they fit in with their hopes and dreams for their family lives? What about the things they love to do outside of work?

You can start this growth plan with a brand new employee as soon as they start with you – even introduce it at the interview stage.

For existing employees, introduce it to the team at a significant point of the year – say, at the end of the financial year, or just after New Year. In appraisals, find out where their passions and energies lie that are not necessarily tapped during their working day. The key here is to come up with a unique plan for each member of the team. If it isn't unique, it's less likely to work.

The onus does not have to fall entirely on you to find out what makes your team tick. Think laterally … introduce a regular informal lunch hour or early evening get together where each of them can offer a short presentation on what they love to do outside of work, or an unusual skill.

You know the old adage, "Those who play together stay together". It happens to be true. Allow them to get to know each other beyond their working roles and you'll see some magic start to happen. This is a wonderful opportunity to highlight and break some bad habits, too, without shining the spotlight on anybody. The urge to learn from each other and mould together as a team can iron out a lot of crinkles in an individual's sales practices that might otherwise take you hours one on one.

Set up a mentorship programme in-house. This takes buy-in from everybody, but it's worth exploring and setting up, even on an informal 'buddy system', as it's been proved time and time again that both the mentor and mentee benefit psychologically and, ultimately, in their respective careers.

Once you know what makes each of your team members tick, you will be in a strong position to quietly suggest and encourage partnerships of this kind. You will be amazed at the results. According to studies, seventy-five per cent of executives say that their mentors helped them to achieve their current position at work. The kind of bonding and sharing that happens on an informal yet deep human level creates a happier and more productive workplace. Try it!

CHAPTER 6
TAKE YOUR TIME WITH EACH TEAM MEMBER

"A good listener is not only popular everywhere, but after a while he knows something."

-Wilson Mizner

Creating a team that loves to work as one takes time, patience and a lot of attention to detail. I'm not talking about the job itself, here. There's something very important that needs your attention on an ongoing basis if you want your people to stay with you. In a word, it's *nurturing*.

Does that sound old-fashioned? I hope so … there's a lot to be said for yesteryear's values and courtesies. Your team members might have every tool for the job at their disposal, easy working hours and unbeatable salaries, but nothing will keep them from leaving if they're unhappy.

It's true that not every telemarketing company bothers with team nurturing. In such a fast-paced, results-driven marketplace, who has time for it?

There's an easy answer to that: nobody does. The best team leaders *make* time for it, though. They know that the happiness and welfare of the team is top priority. Without it, results will slip as performance dwindles; in all likelihood, staff turnover will be high and costly.

If you're thinking, "I know that it's important but I really don't have the resources to spend more time on the team unless it's on calls", then think again. You cannot afford *not* to spend time on the team. Each member, individually. It's vital that you spend time to understand each person intrinsically.

Developing, cherishing, supporting and encouraging others doesn't come naturally to everyone, though. There's really no shame in your feeling a little intimidated at the prospect of having to get to know everybody personally.

For some, getting to know and care about others is easy; for many, it's a challenge and can make you feel anxious. If you fall somewhere in between the two, this part of the book will give you some ideas of how and where to start with your own team. You'll gain some insights as to how treating each of your people as an individual will improve your business.

Bespoke Treatment

Not surprisingly, there's no 'one size fits all' trick to nurturing your team. Humans are complex creatures; despite our differences, though, we all respond similarly to kindness and care.

You're looking for a good 'fit' when it comes to recruiting and keeping your staff. Consider, if you will, how you would go about dating somebody new: you'd be curious about this person and eager to find out everything you could about them to see if they'd be a good match for you. Where do they come from? What do they do for fun? What kind of movies do they watch? What's their favourite meal? How do they dress? The questions are endless – as long as you're interested. When you lose interest, you stop asking questions.

The key is to *get interested* in your team. Where do they go when they've finished work? Who has family? Who lives alone? All of these questions take time to have answered; you need to find the way that works best for you to spend time with each person.

The natural time to start the process is right at the very beginning of your relationship – at the recruitment stage. That's the perfect opportunity to pose a few questions to the candidate that have nothing to do with the job at hand. You'll probably find that this has the added benefit of helping them to relax during the interview, too.

Regular one-to-one meetings and appraisals are not necessarily good times for informal conversation. These times should remain focused, providing a safe forum for both of you to discuss work issues. Rather, create unscheduled 'breaks' for yourself when you can be amongst your team, listening and paying attention.

Some companies try to short cut the organic process of 'getting to know the team' by issuing psychometric tests. Pages and pages of questions are handed out to each new recruit for them to fill in, asking them all sorts of personal things in pursuit of discovering their 'personality type'.

This kind of testing may be useful in

psychologist's practices but they're not helpful in the workplace. Firstly, most people admit to their feeling pressurised and anxious as they fill in their answers. Many suspect that management has a hidden agenda and try to second guess the 'right' or 'wrong' answer, rather than simply responding with the truth. In this way, the test can give you a false reading. In reality, you'll never really know if you're being told the truth or not. Everybody's time can be saved by simply sharing a conversation.

Secondly, the answers that your staff member gives may respond so directly to the question that you miss out on discovering other skills or personality traits that they might have. With a little more information, such as is usually naturally offered in a conversation, you could discover a few hidden pearls of wisdom or pleasant surprises in your team member.

As time goes on and with regular interaction and interest on your part in your team, you'll start to observe each person's 'softer' skills. As everybody is unique, make it your aim to discover the full range of soft skills within your team so that you can really encourage them to work in the way that suits them best, complementing and supporting each other.

Very often, we make the mistake of focusing on the big stuff and we forget the detail. Taking care of the little things that make a person happy at work can generate the biggest results over time and a strong, cohesive team.

Several months ago, I took on a new recruit who had come from a large telemarketing company that is known for getting top sales. After her first week with us, she had bonded with the team and said she absolutely loved her new job.

"Didn't you have a strong team where you were, then?" I asked.

"It was alright but nothing like this," she laughed. "When we hit our last sales target, management gave each of us a bottle of Prosecco but not one of us wanted to share it with anyone from work. There was no real sense of teamwork for me. This one feels like a family."

That is exactly what I like to hear. If you can establish a team that feels like a family, they'll stay with you.

You might already have a team that's formed from people with varying habits. Where do you start to improve its uniformity in call quality when you have team members who have been doing the job this way for two or three years already?

'Rewiring' Staid Team Members

It is always difficult to get good people to stay. That's why I put so much time into building the sense of camaraderie within our team, giving them far more of a reason to stay than they could ever find to leave.

If you can get your people to feel playful at their work as much as they're moving forwards, they will want to stay with you. They need to know that they matter and have a significant role to play in the team, regardless of their job title. Of course, everybody knows that ... but it's amazing how few managers really take it to heart and act on it consistently.

Simply, we start at the very beginning. We ask them the same questions we ask our new recruits:

"Why do you want to be here?"

"What matters to you?"

We remind them why they're still with us and what that means. When they have a clear picture of the here and now, we then help them to visualise where we are going together and what that will mean for them.

We do this in one-to-one KPI sessions and monthly appraisals with every single agent. These KPIs are not just those that are linked to the number of calls they make, wrap time, positive responses and so on: they include some softer, personal targets, too. I ask each team member to complete a piece of self-development work once a month away from the office.

"I want you to sit down this weekend and watch 'The Wolf of Wall Street'," I'll say, or I'll recommend a book or something similar. It needs to be something different to sending them on a work-related course.

Afterwards, they come back to me and I ask them what two things they took away from the experience, and how they can apply what they've learned to their role. Did they pick up on the character's tenacity in the movie? How did the heroine of the novel overcome the obstacles she had to face? Often, they remark upon character traits that appealed to them and that they want to grow themselves.

This may seem an unusual training method, but believe me, it works wonderfully to both break the monotony of a repetitive job and also to inspire. Of course, they all get rewards for a 'self-improvement task well done' – a fiver, a pizza or a bottle of something nice for reading the book or watching the movie. Who wouldn't find that fun?

CHAPTER 7
NURTURING THROUGH LISTENING

"Act as if what you do makes a difference. It does."

- William James

Of course, you know the importance of listening to your employees. It's no surprise that the more they feel 'heard', the greater their commitment and investment in their work. As managers, we hear it all the time: we spend a huge amount of time in management training that's geared towards improving our listening skills.

When it comes right down to it, though, not enough managers commit to regular self-improvement and working on this most basic of skills. By using the word 'basic', here, I don't mean 'simple'. Real, engaged, powerful listening is far from simple.

It has a name: *active listening*. It takes a lot of effort; even more that, it takes an impressive EQ, or emotional quotient. The skill of active listening is the bedrock of your relationship with your team. It is quite possibly the most powerful skillset you'll ever have, both in your career and your personal life.

When you can truly hear what your team members are trying to tell you – either with or without words – you will have the power to create the most effective working environment for them. In turn, they will rise to the occasion and appreciate their working lives more.

Your bottom line will improve as a direct result of your efforts.

One of the top management consultancy firms, Deloitte, has listed the four main ingredients needed to establish strong team engagement:

- Hands-on management

- A positive workplace

- Opportunities for career growth

- Trust in leadership

In each of these areas, active listening plays a crucial role. You can't hope to know what sort of career opportunities your team members want unless you ask them and truly listen to their answers.

According to research carried out by Sodexo, less than twenty per cent of employees believe that their line manager will "treat them fairly and make the right decisions". This lack of trust shows that there are not enough active listeners in management. When you really listen, you make your employees feel heard and understood.

Finding Your Team's 'Why'

Why did this person want to join your team?

What motivates that person to make as many calls per day as he does?

Which bits of the job does she not enjoy at all?

How does each member of the team best like to be taught new things?

When you practice 'active listening' with your team, you'll start to hear the answers to these questions. Each has their own style of learning; each person will hear the same instruction differently. Rather than using a 'one size fits all' approach to training your team, develop new ways of teaching the same thing to suit different personality types.

Considering that your team spends about a third of their lives at work with you, they deserve your attention. If you nurture them by listening closely to them and responding to their individual needs and wants, you'll have a tighter, more committed team with shared core values. Yours will be a happy place to work – and that, these days, is a rarity!

'Active listening' promotes engagement on the part of your team and stronger, more longlasting relationships with each of your staff members.

How can you learn to become an active listener?

Active Listening

When you become an 'active listener', you unveil the subtext of what someone is trying to communicate. You learn to 'read between the lines' and discover the full meaning of the message. As a manager, it's one of the most important skills you can have. It's the key to your building stronger relationships with your team.

Instead of merely waiting for a gap in conversation to start sharing your own message, active listening will have you making liberal use of pause and questioning. When you allow yourself time to ask questions of one of your staff members, you unearth a lot more information.

Most people are wary of pause and silences in conversation; we tend to leap in and fill up all of the gaps with more words. Try it yourself when you next have a conversation with someone face to face: leave a short pause after some of their sentences and see how unnerving it can be for both of you! When you get used to it, you will see how useful it is in allowing your brain to process what you've heard properly and to come up with a qualifying question.

Once you've mastered it, you'll become increasingly aware of who is actively listening around you in all kinds of everyday situations – and conversely, who's just waiting to get a word in edgeways.

The normal listening process comprises six

defined stages: hearing, selecting, attending, understanding, evaluating and remembering.

In 'active listening', we include the '*Three As*' in the process: *attitude*, *attention* and *adjustment*. That is to say, you approach the conversation with an open attitude, laying aside any preconceived ideas about what you're about to hear; you listen with curiosity and concentration; you allow your opinions to be altered as a result of what you hear.

Encouraging Team Engagement

All this effort that you're putting into 'active listening' will pay dividends when you see how much happier your team is. A satisfied team that trusts its management will stay rather than run off to the competition.

In practice, you can use 'active listening' to avoid potential problems at work, to motivate each team member according to their goals and to reap the benefit of hearing everybody's ideas for the business. Staff who feel respected and nurtured gain in confidence and like to share their ideas, adding value to their role. How much easier would your job be were you to have such input?

The most obvious and best way to encourage your team to share their thoughts and ideas with you is by holding regular one-on-ones with each team member. This isn't always possible, though, and, depending on the size of your team and where they are based, long periods of time might elapse between meetings with each person.

One way of counteracting that is by setting up new ways for everyone to stay in touch. For example, you might run spot surveys via email for the team, with just one or two questions for immediate feedback. Chat groups on phones and online conferencing are relatively easy to create – and a good old-fashioned suggestion box even more so.

If you ask for feedback, though, remember that you need to implement the suggestions that you approve. Don't wait too long before you take action: your team will be watching to see how their input can influence the decisions made by management. This is a valuable opportunity to reward their transparency and help with a sense of empowerment.

You don't need to worry that you'll have a

host of new problems to deal with once you start encouraging your team to open up with you about what makes them happy at work. Generally, people have concerns over unsurprising things, such as commuting time, pay, skill shortage or overtime. These are all manageable, posing no unique problem for you as a manager. The important part of this process is that you are perceived to be listening to each of them, which will help them to feel nurtured.

Everybody likes to feel cared for. When your people do, they will want to stick with you through thick and thin.

Top Tips to Becoming an Active Listener

1. Stay focused on the conversation. Ignore others while your companion is speaking, looking them straight in the eye.

2. Don't interrupt and allow pauses to fall naturally – breathing spaces in the conversation.

3. Ask questions about what they're saying rather than trying to get your own point of view heard.

4. Your body language should say, "I'm interested". Lean in slightly, use open gestures with your hands and relax your shoulders.

5. Until the other person has spoken, don't assume you know what they're going to say.

6. Reassure your companion that whatever is said will be kept private – and make sure you keep that promise. Without trust, you can't hope for a strong relationship with your staff.

7. Make a note of what was important to the other person afterwards. It is important to remember not just what a person says but how they say it, too. When you refer to the conversation again sometime in the future, it will demonstrate how well you listened and make your team member feel valued.

CHAPTER EIGHT
A FOUNDATION OF RAPPORT

"Great things are done by a series of small things done together." - Vincent van Gogh

Your capacity to encourage and teach your team consistently is crucial for its wellbeing. Which kind of a leader are you? Do you dominate your team and push them forwards with rules and regulations, or are you more liberal and open to active listening?

The old days of enforcing one's superiority on a team are long gone. Now, people simply vote with their feet if they're unhappy. Whichever way you lead is up to you – but you can't do both. You are either committed to the old-fashioned, demanding form of rule or to the more modern, liberating approach. Otherwise, you will end up giving your team mixed messages and failing to secure anyone's respect.

Encouragement is one of the key features of modern leadership. There are many ways to incentivise someone to stay and evolve as part of your top telemarketing team other than by using business-related credits.

Once you know each of your team members personally and you've spent time discussing their own goals in one-to-ones and appraisals, you will have a much clearer idea of what motivates them. By helping them to break down their 'Five Year Plan' into smaller, more achievable tasks, you will encourage them to stay with you longer. This in turn gives them more opportunities to shine, resulting in a self-perpetuating cycle of positive growth.

It all starts with you and your initial decision and commitment to build a foundation of rapport with each of your team members.

Clear and Open Lines of Communication

It's so important to keep the team in close communication – not just with you but with each other. Many problems can be minimised or avoided altogether when everyone is on the same page. You can offer training in this area, but if you've recruited someone who already has innately strong communication skills then you've spared yourself a headache.

Ask them for their help from time to time – encourage them to use their softer skills. It can boost self-esteem and a person's sense of belonging immeasurably to know that they're valued by the rest of the team not just as a worker, but as a unique individual, too.

'Problem solving', 'emotional control' and 'purpose' are the top three 'soft skills' that all of us need to know more about at work. Your team needs these soft skills as they boost staff retention and encourage a sense of company culture. These are not innate qualities, mind you; virtually none of us has them naturally. We all learn them – managers and staff alike. It's well worth your time and budget to invest in an expert's training for your team in these areas – not once off, but on a regular basis. You'll see the results on the bottom line soon enough.

Making Decisions and Facing the Outcome

If you're not naturally a decisive person, this can be difficult to overcome. However, your ability to make decisions and to stick to them can be vastly improved with practice. Your decisions might not please everyone, but they're yours to make and you're not out to try to please everyone in any case.

When you make decisions that affect your team, make them with empathy, remembering what you know about the people around you and what makes each of them tick. For example, with a new starter, do the fact find about their personality, their habits, loves, hobbies and hopes for the future … the 'Five Year Plan'.

I find using small gifts from time to time helps to cement the relationship and makes a person feel special … who doesn't like a little gift or token of thanks every now and then? Keep them small and understated at first – you can move on to bigger things like a special hamper or day out later, when they've been with you for long enough to really feel like family.

Authenticity

There needs to be authenticity running throughout your company – on every level.

Although it's not always possible to know every

single detail of every job that's carried out by your team, you should make sure that you know each person's job as intimately as possible, especially those whom you specifically line manage. It cuts out the 'us and them' kind of thinking, diminishes the chances of someone's taking credit for somebody else's work and makes you a part of the team, while affording you respect in your role as a leader.

Don't take on a customer you wouldn't be prepared to handle yourself. Your integrity is being scrutinised daily by your team. If you behave with sincerity, you will not have to work for others' respect. You'll have more of their attention in the one-to-one settings as a result and an increase in their commitment to improve.

Genuine Interest

You can't fake this. You either have the energy ready to invest in other people or you don't. That doesn't mean, though, that because you might feel a little discouraged from time to time you can't find the energy and excitement within you to get alongside your team again and encourage them.

Others respond to positive energy and motivated decision making. You need to remind yourself several times a day about why you're developing your dream team – you can fall in love with your business everyday that way. The more charisma you share in the office, the better everyone's response to you will be.

Bring this charisma to each member of your team in regular appraisals and one-to-ones. Help them to get the brief right so that they know your standards of how to service your client.

New starters benefit from plenty of energetic interaction from you. Generally, in the industry, they're handheld for days when they first begin in a new role and are then suddenly left alone to work things out and get on with the job. Without consistent support, the kind of bad habits that we talked about in Chapter Four will set in.

To avoid that, have weekly team chats and on an individual level, five minutes of one-to-ones and feedback every single day. Yes, that is a major commitment. If you want that top team that will stick with you, though, you have to nourish it. This is how you do it and what will make you not just a good manager but an excellent one. Not only will your team stay with you, but also you'll attract the better candidates for new roles as your reputation spreads.

Remember that no two people can concur on everything all the time. Individual members of your team are sometimes not going to agree with you, either. That's alright: they have a right to their ideas and feelings. The kind of working environment that you're working so hard to provide them is the very reason that they are encouraged to air their views in the first place. Issues will come up and there will be the odd disagreement, of course. It's inevitable.

Don't be afraid of letting those happen – they're natural and a part of the normal growth of a good team. With open communication and a culture of empathy and active listening throughout the team, you will get over this and move on collectively to see new victories very soon.

PART 3
AUTHENTIC
TRAINING

CHAPTER NINE
EVERYBODY LEARNS DIFFERENTLY

"High expectations are the key to everything."
-Sam Walton

A new recruit who joined us recently told me during a feedback session about her previous place of work.

"I thought it was a good place to be," she said, picking her words carefully. "I couldn't imagine that there would be so much more to telemarketing than being rewarded with a usual bottle of prosecco on hitting your call target. But this – this has been a really amazing first week. You've all been so attentive and have really made me feel like I'm included and wanted here. It feels like I'm a part of the family – after just seven days!"

It was the first time that she'd experienced a real sense of 'team'.

Sometimes we forget to look at the little things when it comes to our recruits as we look at the big things. Yes, she had joined us to fulfil a goal, but not just for now. She has a life to live and needs longer term goals to live it in the most fulfilling way possible.

We want her to go on doing that, and for that to happen, she needs to feel accepted by the team and wanted from the start. She has to be treated like a person in her own right, not just as a means for the company to achieve a sales target.

If you want to keep good people on your team, you have to learn how to get the best from them and how to keep them engaged by showing them the best of themselves. After all, you want to avoid the staff turnover churn.

Getting to Know Your Team as Individuals

Nurturing is not just about training, showing staff how to stick to their personal development plan and giving feedback. It's also about really taking the time to understand each member of your team individually and what makes them tick.

Neither you nor your team members should

assume that success in telemarketing is all about money. Job satisfaction, feelings included, is extremely important to people.

There's only one way to find out what triggers a person to feel involved and happy in a sales environment, and that's by talking to them.

"Why Did You Want to Join Us?"

When you look at somebody's CV and you see that they've had ten jobs in the last two years, you can't help but be circumspect about employing them. Why did they keep jumping ship?

Until you ask them, you cannot know the real reason – and it's all too easy to jump to the wrong conclusion. They might not be non-committal or untrained at all; it might be that they simply felt undervalued and excluded from the team.

The match between a recruit and a business cuts both ways: not only does the new staff member have to be right for the task at hand but the business has to be right for them, too - in its ethics, core values and personality fit.

It's up to you to find out "Why did they leave

their last job? What can we do better, and what are we going to do better in order to keep them?" When you can answer those questions, you can begin to come up with a tailor-made training plan for each team member.

One size does not fit all. I am not a fan of using one training programme for an entire salesteam. Every conversation with each individual is different. None of us is a robot, so it stands to reason that we learn best in our own, unique way.

Authentic Training for Each Team Member

As you read earlier, everybody likes to learn differently. Similarly, every business operates differently. I like to encourage my team to ask me questions about all kinds of things to do with the way the business operates. The transparency that this fosters gives rise to really positive ties with each team member as it helps them to feel a part of the whole.

People need to understand the purpose of why they're being asked to do something. As I've seen, this is far more valuable to them than a bottle of prosecco for a short-term sales target hit.

As you get to know each of your team members, you might find it useful to keep a list of personality traits which can prompt you in what to look for. None is wrong or right – they're simply common human characteristics that, once you're aware of them, can help you to draw alongside your team member and use the right cues to nurture them onwards.

PERSONALITY ATTRIBUTES AND TRAITS

Communication traits

- Persuasive – tone of voice and emphasis are important here.

- Awareness – in discussion or negotiating situations

- Articulate – being clear and making the complex straightforward

- Focused – keeping to the point and what you're trying to achieve

- Charismatic – making the right impression, getting attention and people listening

- Emphatic – where it counts, not in a contradictory way.

Character Traits

- Confident – no clear doubts, otherwise they'll lack credibility

- Tenacity – if it's a real opportunity, don't let go of it!

- Enthusiastic – this can be contagious and help influence others

- Clear-headed – otherwise can get thrown off-course

- Conscientious – trustworthy, doing it right and being reliable

- Courageous – helps ability to be effective in unexpected situations

- Genuine – contributes in so many ways and can give credibility

- Cooperative – agreeable, but without giving all the profits away

- Friendly – without being over-friendly and creating barriers

- Grit / Determination – that real drive to keep going and achieve.

Awareness Traits

- Knowing when to be proactive and take the initiative

- Observant – don't miss useful clues

- Perceptive – helps with the clues for understanding people.

Attitude Traits

- Optimistic – persistence when rejected, and handling setbacks better

- Passionate – passion leads to persuasion

- Results orientated – without this, where's the drive?

- Resourceful – active in difficult situations and come up with solutions

- Hardworking – getting the job done and going 'that extra mile'

- Insightful – can understand what's behind what is being said and done.

Working Traits

- Organised – helps get more done
- Realistic – not getting carried away
- Respectful – lack of respect is a Sales killer
- Thorough – helps hanging on in there
- Winning – a winner has confidence

Team Attributes

- Good team player – can influence others
- Always reliable – setting a good example
- Always positive – even when something has gone wrong
- Open-minded and co-operative – helps changes to work
- Friendly and business-like - with ability to gain respect
- Shows commitment – to winning with the team
- Takes a constructive approach – helps to cope with any ups and downs

- Accepting - that no job is too small

- Tactful – careful how they phrase things

- Putting points across effectively - shares knowledge and information with the team

- Making right impression - getting attention and people listening

The Magic Wand

I hate to disappoint you but there isn't one. The closest thing to it, though, is this simple act:

Always ask your team member to repeat back to you what they've understood you to say after a training session.

They will repeat back to you what they understood you to say – not necessarily what you did say. That's when you can discover:

- how you can improve on expressing yourself

- how they listen

- how they process information that they've heard.

That is without a doubt the most helpful 'magic wand' you can use – and the more frequently the better! It will save you an enormous amount of pain and time. No two people process the same information in exactly the same way.

Note – you're not asking them to repeat back to you what you said. You're asking them to tell you what they *understood* from your words. It will take you just a few seconds to ask them the question, but believe me, it will save you hours later.

There are many ways to get to a goal.

Bespoke Teaching

In Chapter Twelve we look at how you can set the KPIs for so many different individuals. I strongly suggest, though, that you let each individual have time to learn not just their job but your business too, before you start judging them on their KPIs.

Don't judge a book by its cover; when you give things time to develop, you understand the person. A human behaves very differently to a robot and you can't learn very much about a person through personality profiling as it is too blanketed.

Some people can be very good at pulling the wool over your eyes in the early days, too. If you have a sharp gut instinct, you'll be better off judging if a person is a fit for your team and vice versa by that.

We can't learn something new unless we are conscious that there is a gap in our knowledge. If your new team member doesn't know that their delivery sounds flat on the phone or that they're consistently missing a cue at a certain point in their script or project sheet, they won't have a hope of fixing it.

They can only fix what they know they should. You carry the responsibility of enlightening them to what they don't know – not in a negative, punishing way, but in an inspiring one that leads to new opportunities for growth and self-development.

There may be several things that you know you can bring to their attention, but as I say, people learn best when they are asked to concentrate on one or two things at a time. Don't ask them to multitask as it simply is not effective when it comes to learning.

People are generally better at knowing facts,

such as what to say in response to a given cue, than recognising their own behaviours. While a telemarketer might know what to say in response to a 'no' from a prospective buyer, they might not be aware that they become forceful when they respond due to fear of losing the sale.

This lack of self-awareness can keep a person stuck in a rut, unable to move forward and improve unless you step alongside them and guide them through. Sometimes, their simply being made aware of what they didn't know about their own behaviour can be just the thing they need to initiate positive change. You might not have to break anything down further than that in order to see some wonderful results.

As with our new recruit who felt like she'd just found a team that felt like family, a sudden revelation can come as a real surprise to someone. Depending on how you deliver it, of course, it can be either a truly happy experience or one that they'll always want to forget.

You have the ability, honour and responsibility to nurture each one of your team: it's a privileged position that you're in and this ability to shape and help someone to evolve is a powerful one. Be aware of that always and commit to handling it ethically – never, ever consciously abuse it.

Sometimes, they might say, "Of course! I knew that already!" or words to that effect. What they're alluding to is their latent, instinctive knowledge – and they may well have known what they're now seeing consciously on an unconscious level. When this happens, all the better – as they will never forget this new learning. Its imprint is so much stronger than a memorised fact.

It follows that the more self-aware your team members are and the more aware they are of not just what happens around them but why they happen, the stronger and happier each of them will be. The synergy of everybody working in and experiencing such an encouraging, evolving arena will take your team to another level entirely.

Your Responsibility as a Leader

It takes a brave individual to decide at the start of a process that they will be answerable for every action of an employee that leads to a reaction from a customer. Yet as your own business owner, that's what you did the moment you recruited your first telemarketer.

It might not feel very comfortable reading it like that, but it's true. Most of us fall short of the 'perfect boss' title as we're human. None of us is perfect.

One of the most prevalent ways we let ourselves and our teams down is by our dodging responsibility for the awkward things that happen. We blame other things.

"The client didn't give us enough information on the target market …" or, "So and so said that they had five years' experience in selling IT products – they should have been able to make that sale …" or even, "Our team meeting will have to be postponed as too many of the staff are behind in their calls".

We like to use these kinds of statements because it lets us off the hook – it's something else's fault rather than our own. In every case, the truth is being thinly disguised by the excuse. The truth really is that you should have trained your staff to take more accurate briefs from the client and to double check the information about the target market … you should have sat with the new, 'experienced' recruit to see for yourself if he could sell IT products ... and you should have made sure that the whole team stayed on track and prioritised the team meeting.

It's only when we own up to this pattern of blaming other things or even other people for things not going as well as we'd like in our business that we are able to change our ways.

When we take on responsibility properly, we start doing things differently. We really 'step up' to meet each challenge and start to behave like proper leaders. It does not just take one, big decision, mind you. We have to decide to 'step up' time after time, day after day.

In each challenging situation, big or small, we can ask ourselves the important question, "What else can I do that will change this result?". As long as we take action to change things, we will get different results.

CHAPTER TEN
YOUR TEAM'S HIGH EI

"If you don't give up on something you truly believe in, you will find a way." - Roy T. Bennett

It's no wonder that Emotional Intelligence (EI) is regarded to be on of the top skills you can own in business. When you are able to perceive, understand, manage and control your own feelings and emotions, you're in the driving seat of your day to day experience.

Your EI is the key tool you will use as you work towards more solid relationships with the members of your telemarketing team. If you have a decent EI quotient, you'll have a realistic understanding not just of your own strengths, weaknesses and personality traits, but of those of your team, too. Seeing as retaining your staff is your main goal, it's plain that your Emotional Intelligence quotient needs to be high and in great working order. It's no longer enough for an employee or manager to have a high enough IQ for the job: they have to have a high EI, too.

The most successful business teams these days are those that are able to adapt quickly to new conditions and situations. As a case in point, since the pandemic, many businesses that were unable to rethink their practices and adapt overnight to an online platform were hit very badly. Those that made it through were those that had teams that could think creatively, move as one and take decisive, brave action largely due to their shared high EI.

The good news is that it is not reserved for the lucky few. It's a skill that can be learned and improved. With your EI leadership, your team will become the one that other telemarketing companies want to have.

Out With the Old Ways of Management

The old 'rule by fear' style of management finally disappeared as the dust settled after the Second World War. Back then, management of most companies quite literally comprised demobbed officers from the war, so it was hardly surprising that orders were barked and the staff scuttled about, terrified and hiding their insecurities.

There's no use for that kind of behaviour in the workplace now, but it's certainly taken the business world long enough to figure out what it needs instead.

I believe that people have a basic right to their being made to feel happy, included and important in their workplace. I am committed to making sure that everyone in my team finds moments of fun, excitement and exploration in their daily work lives as it brings out the best in them and the team as a whole. I encourage each of them to think for themselves and to be proactive and they are, in turn, committed to the team and take pride in their work.

The amount of time and money an autocratic, 'command and control' style of management can cost a company is huge. A telemarketer's job is by nature repetitive and can easily become dull … anybody with that job role in a stifling, authoritarian company would be daft not to leave at the earliest opportunity.

Do you encourage your team to use their

Emotional Intelligence by using yours?

Encouraging Your Team to Use Emotional Intelligence

This isn't about letting standards slacken or your wanting to make best friends out of all of your team members. You need to retain their respect. At the end of the day, your business is there to make money and it just so happens that encouraging a healthy EI quotient in your team is the most effective way to do it. Added to that the human factor of how good it is for your people's psychological wellbeing, it seems to me to be a no-brainer that this is the way to go.

It makes sense that if you have a healthy EI, you will be more able to relate to the needs of your team with empathy which will affect your decision-making for the better.

HOW YOUR BUSINESS WILL BENEFIT FROM A GREATER USE OF EI

Culture

If you have empathy towards your staff, you will see a good productivity on a daily basis. Your nurturing them has the effect of making them want to do better, to reach better results.

Instead of using the 'stick' to chase them on from behind, you're using the far more empowering 'carrot' to lead them from the front. The whole 'feel' of the culture at work will be one of positivity and progress.

Sharing of Ideas

Although you are in charge, you are neither infallible nor a font of all wisdom and creativity. You simply can't expect to be the one to come up with all of the new ideas. With EI, you can encourage others to think creatively and contribute their ideas regularly for the good of the team. They learn so much from each other by this interchange.

Independently Driven

Generally speaking, those with a higher EI tend to be more independent, self-regulated and able to use initiative. What's more, they don't rely on external sources to motivate them to do better ... they like to do that themselves. From setting their five-year plans to managing their one time in and out of work, these are the kinds of talents you can expect your Emotionally Intelligent team to have.

Knowing that, how much easier would it be for you to work with them on their personal goals in conjunction with your company's core values?

Physical Benefits

There have been many studies in recent years on the impact of stress on mental and physical health. In short, it impacts on both very heavily. Heart disease, blood pressure, depression and anxiety are all inarguably aggravated by stress.

Wellbeing and the new, rather more 'woke' *wellness* has rightly become a focus of work these days. Anybody with a relatively high EI understands why. Apart from the human factor of pain and suffering, the huge cost of sick leave and absenteeism costs businesses thousands every year.

With a happy team comes a happy daily life in the workplace – with none going off sick unless they genuinely are.

At the end of the day, you want a team that really enjoys being together as one. If each of your team members follows your lead and nurtures the others, you have done your job. Compassion and empathy in the telemarketing arena are not universal … those of us who know how much Emotional Intelligence can inspire and animate a call sales environment swear by it. Connecting and interacting with each other on a human, nurturing level – one that implies, "You're important to me," – will always bring the best out of each person.

Your reputation will go before you, too. You will be seen as a top team to work with as you have successfully created a positive environment for everybody. Your high team EI is most certainly something well worth striving for.

PART 4
BACK TO BASICS

CHAPTER ELEVEN
CLEAR COMMUNICATION WITH YOUR CLIENT

"Learn from the mistakes of others. You can't live long enough to make them yourself."
- Eleanor Roosevelt

Earlier, I addressed some of the 'bad habits' that can emerge in the early days of a new telemarketer's role as a part of your team. Sometimes, though, it's the clients themselves who pose challenges.

Usually, it's because they haven't tried telemarketing before and so haven't a clue as to what to expect during the process. Sometimes, it's because they've had a little experience with telemarketing either with an external company or an in-house team, and they now think they know your job better than you do. Occasionally, you might come across someone who has had no experience and yet still thinks that they know your

130

job better than you do.

In my experience, "The customer is always right" is not true. The customer very often needs managing just as much as your team. In the rarest of incidents, I've actually turned a project away as I could not align our core values and way of working to what the customer said that he wanted us to do.

If you find yourself compromised, listen to your instinct and never feel pressured to take on a project that does not 'fit' your team or your brand image. It isn't worth it in the long run as word travels fast.

Some of the kinds of customer behaviours I've faced with my team over the years might crop up in your career, too:

- *Scaremongering*

  A customer once wanted us to use scare mongering as a technique to win new business. I found this highly unethical. People should buy from you because first and foremost they like you and resonate with what you are offering, not because they have been petrified into buying. I turned this project down.

- *Over Briefing*

Customers sometimes want us to know all of the ins and outs of their product before we picked up the 'phones.

While to some customers it might seem counter-intuitive, we really do not need to know every single detail about the product or service to do our job, much less the customer's company. This is a case of over-briefing, which takes firm management.

Tell the customer that you will ask the questions to get the concise, perfect brief that you need to get the best results for them. Don't let them waffle on about things that you can't use during the task and ask them to condense any written information they give you which is not applicable. They're paying for your time – so point out to them that this is money down the drain.

- *Lack of Sales Knowledge*

It's not at all necessary for a customer to be experienced in sales. In fact, it can be a real blessing if they're not, as taking on a customer who thinks they know about sales and yet who

132

clearly has never heard of the sales cycle or how long it takes to build a relationship with prospective buyers can be a headache.

Again, this kind of customer needs some positive managing, especially in the early days. If you can point out clearly and calmly that you are the expert in this field and they accept that, you're on good ground.

However, if they don't accept that and continually try to tell you your job, you might have to cut ties before you get too far into the process. As they say, you can take a horse to water ...

• *Dictating the Script*

It's difficult to tell before you take a project on just how involved the customer wants to be in writing the 'script', or 'project sheet'. Quite often, despite their having delegated the sales task to you, they insist on telling you what to put in the script. They try to force you to add the things that they want to say, rather than what their prospective buyers want to hear.

Just as in the above example, you will need to be firm and manage the situation positively when you get to this stage.

It can be helpful to say something like, "I know that you understand and know your product/service more intimately than anybody. In order for us to produce the tightest script that will get you the best results, I would suggest that you take a step back from the process at this stage as you might be too 'close' to it – like an artist needs to step back from his work sometimes."

It might sound a little overegged, but it flatters and still makes sense. Nobody's feelings can be hurt when they're being compared to an artist, after all!

Every client has his own preferred way of having telemarketers communicate with customers and that is to be expected. In the main, you will be able to work with what a client who has experience with telemarketing requests of you.

For example, they might say, "I don't want you to leave a voicemail", or "There is no limit to the number of times you need to call a company to get an answer". They might prefer a strict 'three call rule', after which you don't call a fourth time irrespective of whether or not you've made contact with the decision maker. Even "Hound them until you get a definite 'yes' or 'no' ..." is still a plausible request – there are many, many variables. It depends on the brand of the business and how the client wants to be perceived by those on the receiving end of the calls.

It's your job, though, to make it clear to a client new to telemarketing that it's his brand that will be judged by those receiving the calls, not your telemarketer. Once a new client understands that, they'll usually be happy to concede to your opinion and follow your advice.

We start off by asking a customer, "In a single sentence, can you tell me what you do?" Very often, they can't. They need help with their message – and this comes out in the scriptwriting stage.

Next, we find out from the customer why it is that they think that telemarketing would help them. Often, the people we're working for are not sales people. They're often technical people, or creative people. They know their product or service inside out but they can't sell it to others. If it's an inbound inquiry, though, they'll be happy to take orders all day long.

These requests are what clients come to us with. We, however, have one standard: we don't stop until we get a qualified conclusion – either a 'yes' or a 'no' from either the decision maker or main influencer. It's not done through aggression – it's done through our being politely persistent.

Transparency of Deliverables

Before you take the brief, you need to determine what it is that the client is expecting to achieve at the end of the process.

A typical type of client that hires a telemarketing company has a huge salesteam but doesn't want to manage the churn in-house.

Another is the kind that needs the old-fashioned door-knocking, relationship-building that might take five years to make a sale: the campaign is more about their branding over time. They might be one of three companies in the country who are selling a specific product, so they have a one in three chance of getting the work.

For the latter, the telemarketing is all about

'top of mind awareness' – establishing that people know who they are for when the lead eventually needs them. Instead of a direct selling campaign, it's more of a slow growing relationship, when we politely remind them over time that "We're still around" so that, in a few years' time, they'll remember us.

You should be able to tell whether a product or service requires a longer, building relationship from the start by the category of business it falls into. There are some products and services about which you simply cannot force a conversation.

For example, we have recently worked on two campaigns at the same time: one was with an accountant and the other with a company which modernises old data systems.

The latter isn't a service that's easily recognisable by the majority of people as something that their business immediately needs. It's only when something goes wrong with their own system processes that they might acknowledge that it needs fixing. Essentially, we're selling a service that people don't even know that they need. It's a tough call …

If they have had no real sales experience before, your client needs to be shown that the people who are going to make the decisions to splash out a hundred thousand pounds for a brand new system are not the ones who are going to be picking up the phone.

In these kinds of cases, I use a blended approach: a mixture of different methods of reaching the decision maker. Before we can get into the 'lead generation' side, we need to cultivate the relationship.

In one instance, we decided to interview our customer's customers, asking them, "What did you buy from us?" and "What problem did it solve for you?" before we got on the phone to sell the campaign product. It was a very useful, informative exercise which also taught us how to use their kind of language, which always helps a sale.

Believe me, this type of relationship-building can take years. I've had customers agree to buy up to five years after I first started to call them and grow the relationship.

A colleague of mine recently had a 'yes' to an accountant who was using her telemarketing team to reach new customers. This is a notoriously difficult category to sell for as people tend to stick with their accountants for years. She put it down to her being in the right place at the right time after having established a long relationship with the new customer: the lead's previous accountant had just retired.

While it's true that certain products and services can only be sold via referrals and rapport building, they do give you credibility over time which is worth a great deal.

We explain to the customer that this isn't your straightforward, day to day telemarketing campaign. I might say, "This isn't a scenario in which I'll make a hundred and fifty calls in a day and get you lots and lots of customers. In this case, I firstly need to cultivate a relationship with the person on the other end of the phone before we can convince him of anything. This takes time – and we need to be very targeted about what it is we're trying to achieve."

Phone Ready in Forty Minutes

Develop a system that checks your team's understanding of the brief – starting with whether this is a quick turnaround, direct sales campaign or a slow churn, relationship building branding campaign.

I have developed a few methods of checking that my team is up to speed over time and can now confidently tell a new client that, given a clear brief, I can have my team "Phone Ready in Forty Minutes". It's not a race, mind you: take your time to check and double check their understanding of the job at hand. If you rush this stage and miss problem areas, you may well end up paying for it with mistakes made once the campaign has launched.

Post-briefing, you might use a multiple-choice quiz with your team to see if they're all clear on the instruction. It's a good way to pull them together and energise them before they get to the phones and it irons out any remaining wrinkles in their understanding of the brief.

Ask your staff, 'What is your understanding of the overall goal?" and 'What does a qualified lead look like to you?". Based on their answers, you'll be able to see very quickly the gaps in their understanding of the brief.

CHAPTER TWELVE
MEASURING AND MONITORING YOUR TEAM

"Our greatest weakness lies in giving up. The most certain way to succeed is always to try just one more time." - Thomas Edison

Deciding on your team's KPIs should be more about what is good for your own team rather than following industry standard practice. What's more, you don't necessarily need six months to get somebody up to speed. Nothing happens all at once, though; you need to focus on one area of training at a time, empathising with each person as a part of your commitment to nurturing your team.

When you take a telemarketer on this journey, work out in advance what the alarm bells will be that you will respond to if things go wrong on the way. Concentrate on listening skills, especially how much time are they spending actively listening on the phone.

An important rule of thumb is to only give them two things to work on simultaneously, for example, how much time they spend actively selling on the phone as opposed to concentrating on rapport building.

You can ask, "What is your definition of a sales indicator on the phone?", and "Why did you spend an extra eight minutes on the phone once they'd got the sales indicator, only to say that there's 'no interest'? What were you talking about?"

Some telemarketers will spend ages on a call, rapport building and talking off topic. Afterwards, they'll enthuse how brilliant the call was when, in fact, they've not inquired about budget, asked who the decision maker is, when the customer is purchasing and so on.

KPIs to Cover

While there are many ways to incentivise an individual based on their personality, of course you need KPIs that apply to the whole team.

As we'll discuss in later, the first thing would be getting the language right on the phone, which is where a properly crafted script or project sheet really helps. After that, though, you should add into your performance measuring and monitoring the following practices.

Repeat Back the Instruction

I would say that three months is ample time for someone to get his head around something. However, we process things better if we're given two things to concentrate on a time.

When you're speaking to someone and you're explaining what the end goal is, you need to be exceptionally clear in your own mind what it is. When you're relaying it to a telemarketer, ask them to repeat what their understanding is of the instruction.

That's the first step - otherwise, you might end up three months down the road wondering why the leads aren't coming in. If it turns out that your telemarketer didn't have a clear understanding of what the campaign was all about in the first place, it will have all been a terrible waste of time.

Time and Motion Study

There are things that you want to do right from the beginning when you allocate a telemarketer to any project. One of the first things my management team and I do is meet all of our telemarketers for what I call a "Time and Motion Study". It focuses on how they think they should spend their time on each call and each step connected with it and then a true calculation of what is feasible.

For example, you could have an expectation of thirty calls an hour. Times that by the number of working hours – say, seven – and your telemarketer should have made about two hundred and ten calls … except that you haven't accounted for how long one person takes to do the administration needed for each call: they need to put their notes in, rewrite from their pad and so on.

Everybody has his own preferred order of doing things, too. So, we sit with the new telemarketer on a call and time them in the first instance how long it takes for them from the point of putting the phone down to populate the system.

I'll warrant, that is a pretty granular process, but we do that only with three people on the telemarketing team and then work out an average for the rest of the team. That's how we gain a more realistic expectation for the newcomer. It's unfair to expect them to be able to operate at the same speed as a telemarketer who's been on the project and a part of the team for months already.

The 'Yes' Response

A KPI that's sometimes left out in telemarketing training to the detriment of the team is what I call 'setting the scene'. Simply, it's "What happens if I get a 'yes'?"

It happens so infrequently for telemarketers that it can come as a surprise and really unseat a less experienced team member. We all know really well what to do when we get a 'no' – we go into 'objection handling' overdrive. As soon as someone says 'yes', though, we forget our lines as we hear 'yes' so infrequently.

To that end, I set a goal of a number of times a new telemarketer repeats a role play training session in their first three weeks, in which a person says, "Yes, I'm interested."

Scorecard

We also sit with them and go through a scorecard which covers all of the important aspects of how a telemarketer makes a call.

It lists a range of factors, from the tone of voice used to whether or not he or she summarised the phone call, did he address the person he was calling correctly, how much time was spent on sales fact-finding and how much time was spent on non-selling.

Each telemarketer gets the scorecard and fills it out according to their estimation of how they've done. Afterwards, the team leader completes it once she's listened to the recording of their phone call.

Needless to say, in the early days there are a lot of discrepancies between the two ... there's often fireworks when we match the two up! After about a month of working together like this, though, the new telemarketer knows what's expected of them.

KPIs are there primarily to guide and coax your team onwards, although they can also really shine a light on whether you've made a good choice of candidate for your team. As much as nurturing your team and matching core values with individual ones helps hugely, sometimes you will have a mismatch.

As we've seen earlier, you need to calculate for yourself when somebody becomes a 'project' and you need to give up on them. Sometimes you can get stuck with someone if you've recruited them through an agency; if you can recruit more organically, so much the better.

Regardless of how enthusiastic they are for the job, if they don't listen properly then you will be wasting your time keeping them on in the long run. The best way you can truly tell if someone is going to work out well as a part of your team is by playing back some of the calls.

Measuring and Monitoring for Call Quality

Sometimes what a person thinks he hears on a call is not what is actually being said. If they waste time repeatedly pushing against a door that will not budge in the conversation with a prospective buyer, it will be evident in the play back. If they are not able to begin to actively listen from then on and to learn from their mistakes after having heard the playback, it's time to part ways.

When it comes to call monitoring, make sure that you judge by 'call connected time' as opposed to 'average call time'.

The latter could be two or three minutes in duration but could comprise a long answering machine message rather than a conversation with a real person. The average 'connected call' records how much time a telemarketer was in real conversation with a person. From that, you can then work out how much time was spent actively selling and how much time was actively *not* selling.

At the end of each day, I ask everyone on the call team to send one good call and one not so good call that they've had to the team leader to listen to. The team leader then provides feedback on those.

It's no good letting the team think that every call they make is good. There's always room for not so good ones, and every individual needs to take ownership of those that they make that could have been improved. As managers, we need to know the bad as well as the good.

For any telemarketer, it's always a bit

cringeworthy to have one of a 'not so good' call dissected in front of you by the team leader, but it's a healthy way to keep tabs on the performance level of the team as a whole as well as per individual. It also, of course, really encourages them to do better next time.

If there genuinely isn't room for improvement on a person's calls, then it's easy for a team leader or line manager to say, "Well done – if you didn't get any leads then it really isn't a reflection on what you're doing. Your calls covered everything and were spot on."

This measuring and monitoring is fundamental for a telemarketer from the very beginning of their journey. After all, this is point at which you set the pace and the tone of their journey with you as a business.

Always Explain 'Why'

I say to all of my staff once a week, "What could we have done better? What did you do that worked particularly well?".

If someone says, "I didn't get many leads this week - the data wasn't great," I'd ask them to qualify their observation, to really look below the surface and find the right evidence.

Recently, I asked a team member, "How many records to you have on your data?"

"Five thousand, and I made five hundred calls."

"So why do you say the data's bad?" I wanted to know.

It turned out that the people he was speaking to weren't the right people – they were not the decision makers.

"Okay – of the five hundred calls you made, how many of the responders weren't the right people for you to speak to?"

"Fifty."

I knew immediately that I couldn't go back to our client and say that fifty out of five thousand people turned out to the wrong ones to speak to. That's just a drop in the ocean – a tiny analysis that isn't good enough to present to the customer. The telemarketer didn't know that, though, and without my asking him I might never have known that he didn't. His recording might always have given me misinformation without that important conversation.

It's about explaining to someone why you do things the way you do. If a telemarketer understands the underlying reason why they're being asked to do something in a certain way, they'll take to the task much better than if they're just told to follow orders. Their understanding of the 'why' very often does away with the risk of the forming of bad habits in the first place.

From that moment on, they will want to do it right and they understand the best way of doing it, rather than just knowing it. It makes a huge difference to performance and team morale.

I can remember an exceptional telemarketer of a certain age who was a little stuck in his ways when he first started with us. He was so used doing things his own way that he didn't make thorough notes in the early days. He'd have a twenty-minute call with someone, and then make half a sentence as a note at the end of the call.

That meant that the line manager had to listen to the full twenty-minute recording of the call to find out what had happened on it. Essentially, that's doubling up on company time for just one call. There's vital information in that call that should have been noted down so that it could have been quickly gone through later.

When I asked him why he hadn't made more notes, he explained.

"Well, I was a manager in a previous role and so I know how to multitask," he said. Firstly, I don't believe in multitasking. Secondly, he needed to get onto the same page as the rest of the team.

The best way to break him of the habit was to break down into time chunks each part of his line-manager's day and present them to him, so that he could see that there was no time for him to spend another twenty minutes listening to the recorded call.

It's much quicker for the line manager to go through a list of bullet points. As he had referred to his previous managerial role, he was able to empathise with that of his own line manager and to respect her method of time management.

Note taking was no longer an unnecessary evil to him; now, it made perfectly clear sense and provided a way for him to help the process overall. The way he felt about being a part of the team and sharing responsibility encouraged him to do his role with more of a team spirit. He understood that he mattered – he wasn't just a number sitting at a desk making calls. He started to take ownership of his role.

There's no question of the chain of events and the 'knock-on effect' somebody's idiosyncratic behaviour can have on the team. That's why you need to explain as early as possible to your team that if they mess up the script or fail to make comprehensive notes, the team leader has to send the call recordings to the customer.

The customer then ticks off the team leader. While responsibility lies with the team leader, the accountability lies with the manager. It would be your duty to call the customer with hands up and a profuse apology. As if that isn't unpleasant enough, you could lose the customer at that point.

Transparency When Things Go Wrong

Happily for me, in over twenty years it's never happened … but it could easily do so. By admitting fault early and being as transparent as possible at all times with my customer, a misguided call has never yet been bad enough to cost me a customer. It lessens the impact if you can truthfully say and prove that you've lost no time at all in calling them to alert them to the potential problem.

"This is what's just happened – it wasn't meant to happen, I'm sorry, Mr Customer". The old saying, "Honesty is the best policy" is certainly true in this kind of unfortunate instance. And remember, everyone is human. Error is a part of our make-up, although there's always an opportunity afterwards to make things right and to improve one's performance so that the same thing doesn't happen a second time.

If you're working with good people, then they will see your credibility rise when you take accountability in front of them.

We have a 'Screw Up Policy' which stipulates that if something goes wrong, come and tell me - don't sweep it under the carpet and hope that it will go away or try to fix it on your own. Come to me and say, "This is what's happened ...".

Then, it becomes a team problem, not one individual's mistake. We tackle it together and get that individual back in the saddle. We care about each other. That caring, team approach goes very far in reducing the number of issues that go wrong. Back up what you're asking for with a reason so that you don't have to justify your requests later and that will help the trust factor to grow.

CHAPTER THIRTEEN
THE "SCRIPT" OR "PROJECT SHEET"

"Life shrinks or expands in proportion to one's courage." - Anais Nin

We come to the meat of the call – the 'script' or 'project sheet' that your callers will follow while carrying out their core task of having a conversation with prospective customers.

Whether you should use a script or not is often hotly debated in telemarketing circles. It's true that a 'read' script can sound utterly insincere, which immediately makes most people on the receiving end of it on their guard and totally distrustful of the caller.

On the other hand, though, 'winging it' or ad libbing too much can lead to disastrous results. If disaster is averted, then there are still usually a few if not several missed opportunities in the call as cues are forgotten.

I choose to do something in between mix the best of both worlds: a 'script' to follow so that no relationship-building opportunity is missed and the freedom for the telemarketer to flaunt their own personality.

Reading Scripts Ad Verbatim

I believe that as each conversation is individual, you don't want to have a script that your telemarketers are all following word for word.

When I've interviewed some people in the past, they've been so rigid about sticking to a script word for word that they can't think 'outside the box' and use their initiative. I came up instead with what I call a "Project Sheet", which comprises guidelines to help the telemarketer to keep the conversation on track rather than a complete script per se. I've included a sample of ours at the end of this chapter.

It's an overview of the objective – how to uncover the goal without delivering a hard sell, word for word manuscript of what they need to say because a natural conversation doesn't flow like a script.

It also allows for nuanced adaptation. After

all, the knowledge of a telemarketer on Day One of a campaign is going to be very different to their knowledge of it a month down the road.

Always tell a client that, although you might not have experience in his business category, the starting point is always the same: the Who, What, Where, When and Why questions have to be answered early.

Over time, I've developed a structured way of asking them so that the information is clear and secured in the earliest stages of the relationship: after that, we enter the client's 'buzzwords'.

There are plenty of books published that deal with the "Who, What, Where, When and Why" questions, so I am not going to focus on those in this chapter. You can find lots of help in those on how to come up with the initial qualifying questions for your own Project Sheet. Here, I am focusing more on the interaction between a telemarketer and the project sheet – how their call experience evolves during their journey in the role.

Project Sheet: Version One

This is for the 'virgin telemarketers' – those on

your team with no experience and those whom you've just taken on. The point of the "Version One Project Sheet" is to qualify the decision maker or, at the very least, the influencer. For any new telemarketer, regardless of background, I always start off with a "Version One" of the Project Sheet which covers the basics.

The assumption is that a caller with experience in the sector is better – but it is still a unique experience to each person. They still have to learn how a client works.

They may be up to speed on a certain product, but brands within a category are very different. Their packages, contract lengths, customer service are different – that's why there are so many businesses in a single category. They are there to service people's different needs and wants.

Go back to basics with every new telemarketer irrespective of their background and go through every category. As they say, "a little knowledge can be a dangerous thing", so nip the small, unwanted habits that a new telemarketer with a little experience brings with them in the bud.

Version One teaches them the terminology to

use throughout the campaign and helps them to set the tone of the delivery that the customer wants to hear.

When the telemarketer's comfortable with that first version, you can add a little more and so on. For example, if it's a technical product, Version One might simply establish who the decision maker is – a very straightforward instruction to "Call this number and ask this question". If that person is not available, then the telemarketers are prompted to ask if there's someone else who can take the call who works alongside the decision maker, or someone else in the same department who deals with these kinds of requests.

Ease them in gently and give them simple things to master from the very start. They will repeat them probably over a hundred times a day, so it really won't take long for anyone in a new telemarketing role to become well-rehearsed on the foundational questions. If these are messed up or left out, the rest of the entire campaign will flounder.

As their confidence grows, you add a bit more to their repertoire so that at no stage in the learning process do they feel over-faced or like giving up.

Remember, a person can only process one or two things at one time; as tempting as it may be to 'fast-track' your telemarketers and get them to the weightier, more complex content of the call campaign, resist the urge. If they have four, five or six things to juggle before they're practiced enough, they're sure to drop a couple of them. Multitasking is a myth: nobody does anything perfectly if there are too many things to focus on at once.

While the opening questions are vital, make sure that your telemarketers spend their early days getting their heads around the language, tone and lingo for best results overall. Also, encourage them to notice and understand the ratio of the number of calls that are not answered, those that are 'not interested' to the 'yes' calls.

The Layout

Organise the information on the Project Sheet in such a way so that the telemarketers can quickly see what the end goal of the campaign. It needs to be broken down into little goals – separate stages with a clear, single objective each time, which together lead to the ultimate end goal.

For example, instead of saying, "I expect you

to get three leads a day", rather say, "Stage One: find out the name of the decision maker. Stage Two: ..." and so on.

Getting the Tone Right

I've never been too keen on tying someone down to prescriptive script because the words might jar with the telemarketer's personality.

When someone is saying something clearly rehearsed, it's patently obvious to the listener that their heart's not in it. It's a red flag to the listener. So, allow your team members to phrase some of their own opening questions. The way they'd each deliver a sentence might be very different to the way you would deliver it.

Personality plays a huge part in this, so your ability to actively listen to each of your telemarketers in the early days of having them work with you is very important. Be sensitive and empathic to your team member's personality and unique way of communicating.

After all, the same message can be delivered in any number of ways: it's not a case of 'it's my way or the highway'. Allow them the freedom and dignity of being able to converse in their own way, as long as they get the correct message across clearly.

Remind them that there needs to be a degree of rapport-building on the call, the amount of which comes down to the brief. This calls for a good balance between IQ and EQ on the part of your telemarketers.

Do you want the aggressive cold call because you've got them so psyched up to be commission-hungry? Or do you want them to gently build a relationship with the customer over time? The Project Sheet or script needs to reflect the longevity of the quality of relationship that you want to build.

Either way, you still need to weave into the script rapport-building terms for the product's features to be showcased. This is where you have to quantify "selling time" versus "non-selling time" on the call. After all, there's 'rapport building' and then there's 'War and Peace'.

Project Sheet: Version Two

When your telemarketers have had their "Version One Project Sheet" for a month, everyone stops looking at it while they're on their calls as it becomes over-familiar.

That's a good time to put it on a flipchart in the call area or change its appearance so that its front of mind again – within vision. The information is all there, right in front of them in a fresh way. A lot of work goes into creating a good "Version One Project Sheet". There's no reason to 'wing it' on a single question.

The format for "Version Two" is the same as "Version One" although the buzzwords are different. The seasoned telemaketers will see the project sheet and know how to break it down and form their questions; the virgin will have to have it broken down into smaller steps – and that takes patience on your part. Give them the assurance that it's okay to take time to do that.

Treasure the Silences

An inexperienced telemarketer usually feels that they have to keep talking to fill silences. It normally comes from nervousness. As you're managing and training using *active listening*, they will learn to allow the pause in time and to let it work for them..

Tricky Responses

There's no doubt that having a script is a quick way to find out where the gaps are in your telemarketer's knowledge and to work out how to help him join the dots.

One of the tricky responses they'll get quite regularly is "No thank you, the product I already have is the best one on the market."

Your telemarketer needs to understand what the most common issues are that people are trying to resolve by purchasing this item.

We're not looking at objection handling or cutting costs, or even whether the prospect wants to buy the product. Rather, we're starting at an earlier point in the process and asking, 'What issues does this product solve?". Start by researching and asking the client for the most common issues in the market regarding the product.

Your telemarketers should be able to work with a project sheet that keeps the conversation moving. Firstly, of course, establish that you're talking to the right person – the one who makes the decisions when it comes to buying the product.

Don't Hear 'No' Where There Isn't One

Nobody likes to be 'sold to'. That's why your telemarketers hear what they think is a 'no' so often. The response might be along the lines of, "Thanks, but we're all sorted out for the year."

That response is not a 'no' by any means. It's an invitation to venture more of an open conversation.

"Okay – that's great," your telemarketer could say. "I'm not trying to sell anything at the moment. For now, I'd like to understand how much you are paying per page and trying to eliminate those hidden expenses for features that don't serve you. They can add up to hundreds of pounds, even thousands over a year."

At that point, your telemarketer can explain what your product does to resolve that issue.

If it's a 'no', it may be 'no' for now, not for forever.

Is There an Obvious USP?

Perhaps the product you're selling is not the cheapest. In that case, find out if you can say with

168

assurance that your product is the best one on the market at fixing a particular problem. If you can say that on your call then that can act as a Unique Selling Point (USP).

You Can't Force a Sale

If yours not the best product on the market for fixing a particular problem, there's no need to try to find another USP.

I go in with the attitude that not everybody is going want to buy, and that's alright. As it turns out, I make more sales with that mindset.

I say, "I'm not trying to sell this to you – it might not be the right product for you," and people like the honesty and integrity of that approach.

That unflustered style has always worked for me, so I stick to it. You can't force a sale. It comes down to finding the balance between a person's IQ and EQ.

I remind myself that it's the decision maker who loses face, remember, if things don't work out after a sale, and often he or she will not want to lose face. So, they'll resist the sale on many levels and it will ultimately come down to price.

Ask for all the information and then explain how the product can help resolve each issue. If it can't, though, I'll hold my hands up and leave the person with a memorable conversation, professionally done.

Establishing a long relationship is often more important than an early sale.

In my experience, it all comes down to building relationships – not just with the client and the buyer, but with the team, too. Establishing and nurturing a relationship with each member of your team is the tried and tested way to create and keep your team – the one you want to have with you far into the future.

As you've seen, it takes time and creativity to do it, but it can be done. If you believe that the rewards are worth it, you have it in you to go the extra mile for the sake of your company. As I say, there's no magic formula; rather, the secret lies in 'going back to basics' and concentrating on validating everyone around you. Just as often as they need to repeat their sales process, you need to repeat your nurturing process.

When you do, you'll see your team become your second family. Enjoy the journey, and may you go from strength to strength together.

EXAMPLE OF A PROJECT SHEET

Project Sheet for Trifle Solutions Ltd

What we do:

We deliver Business to Business (B2B) Telemarketing campaigns to help you generate new business leads, we identify whether other businesses have a need for your products and/or services.

Who to Speak to:

- Head of Sales or Marketing
- Sales Manager

Questions to Ask:

Ask for the named contact on the data, if they are not available ask if they are the correct person to speak with - if not then get the correct name and contact details for whoever is responsible - then ask to be passed through to them.

- Can I ask are you the right person to speak

to who is responsible for new business development? *(listen to their answer)*

- Does your company use telemarketing? *(listen to their answer)* Is this something you outsource, or do you do this inhouse?

- If no – is there any reason for this? Have you done telemarketing in the past? What was the outcome? Do you think it is something your company would consider?

- If yes – are you looking to review your campaign any time soon? When is this likely to be? What is it you look for when deciding on who to use for your campaigns?

Main purpose of call

To identify new prospects for Trifle Solutions.

How we work

We offer our service in two or three stages:

1. Telemarketing trial @ £275 + Vat

2. Telemarketing pilot 3 months

3. 12 month Telemarketing campaign

The telemarketing trial lasts up to three hours. In this time, we ask you a series of questions to understand your company, product and/or related service, before making fifty calls on your data in front of you. This exercise gives you an insight into our service, our deliverability, and our qualification skills. It will also test your data set and identify how receptive your offering is to market.

The telemarketing pilot is a optional step should you wish to dip your toe in the water and outsource telemarketing. This is enough time to build momentum for your campaign and identify your lead cycle. And latterly the campaign itself. We run campaigns over a period of six to twelve months, with a month's notice period clause, i.e., should you wish to pause your campaign at any-time, we require ten working days' notice in writing to put this into effect. During every campaign we make up to one hundred and fifty calls, identifying one to four qualified opportunities.

Details of the Trial.

- **£275 + Vat (Additional travel expenses to be applied if Trifle have to travel to prospects offices) to be paid upon booking. Trial date will not be confirmed until invoice has been paid.**

- Two Senior Account Managers will be in attendance.

- 30/40 minutes will be spent understanding your business and the proposition you wish for us to telemarket. This will form the backbone of the clients campaign.

- Fifty calls made on the data the client provides, in front of the client so that they can see that:

  - Trifle Solutions have understood the client's proposition and can articulate it;

  - Trifle Solutions approach the campaign professionally;

  - How good their data is – this exercise is a good test of the data;

  - And finally it gives an indication of how successful the campaign will be.

- Conclusion of the trial. We discuss the results

of the calls and decide on the next course of action. Client to determine what a "qualified opportunity" is.

Details of the campaign.

- **£7k –** twenty days a month, 14k forty days a month, 21k sixty days a month

- Fourteen days' payment terms.

- Twelve month contract (thirty working days' notice if client wishes to terminate the contract).

- Clients typically use this service on the 14k package

- We make up to one hundred and fifty calls today.

Other services we provide are to be priced on application. These services are:

Data provision.

Printed in Great Britain
by Amazon